W9-BCR-899

THE HISTORIAN AND HISTORICAL EVIDENCE

THE HISTORIAN AND HISTORICAL EVIDENCE

BY

ALLEN JOHNSON

Professor of American History, Yale University

KENNIKAT PRESS, INC./PORT WASHINGTON, N. Y.

THE HISTORIAN AND HISTORICAL EVIDENCE

This edition published in 1965 by Kennikat Press

Library of Congress Catalog Card No: 65-14788

Manufactured in the United States of America

TO

A. S. J.

CONTENTS

PREFACE

To those who believe that literary cleverness and common sense are the only needful equipment for a historian, this book will seem a work of supererogation. Why all this pother about the technique of criticism, the assessment of evidence, and such pedantry? they will ask. Why is it not possible to set down historical happenings just as they occurred? The answer is simple enough to all writers of history who have tried to tell "just how it was" or "how it came to be." Rarely does historical information come to the historian through his own direct, personal observation: it is almost always mediated through some other human intelligence. And so long as human testimony is what it is—subject to all the deflecting influences of time, personality, place, and circumstance—so long must historians learn not only how to collect evidence but how to measure and weigh it. In writing this little book I have had in mind not only future writers of history but that intelligent reading public which would know how to discriminate between histories and histories.

THE HISTORIAN AND HISTORICAL EVIDENCE

CHAPTER I

THE SOURCES OF INFORMATION

One of the incidental results of the World War—would that all were as beneficial!—was a great popular interest in history. The number of journals, memoirs, and histories published exceeded for a time the output of fiction.[1] Never overnice in its choice of books, the general public read pretty much at random, following the line of interest and least resistance. With true journalistic insight, Mr. H. G. Wells floated his *Outline of History* on this rising tide of public interest. The book which he dashed off with characteristic audacity and skill made an instantaneous hit. Even Macaulay in his palmiest days was not so widely read. And Mr. Wells found himself classed in the popular mind among the authori-

[1] Lucian's comment in his introduction to the essay on *The Way to Write History* is very much to the point. "From the beginning of the present excitements—the barbarian war, the Armenian disaster, the succession of victories—you cannot find a man but is writing history; nay, every one you meet is a Thucydides, a Herodotus, a Xenophon. The old saying must be true, and war be the father of all things, seeing what a litter of historians it has now brought forth."

ties on history. Intimations that he really did not belong among the historical immortals were put down as mere indications of professional jealousy. And the man-in-the-street still inquires somewhat petulantly why Mr. Wells is denied his full meed of praise. The query deserves an answer.

It may be premised at the outset that a first-rate historian will wish to go to original sources of information. This Mr. Wells has not done, or done very rarely. He is much like the reporter of an evening newspaper who arrives late on the scene of an accident, after the traces have been removed and the participants dispersed, and who finds himself reduced to the necessity of writing up his story from the accounts published by his rivals in the morning journals. He may hit upon a true statement of the facts, but he can rise no higher than the source from which he draws his information. If it is faulty, his account will in all probability be partial and defective. He must remain a secondary authority.

The matter may be put more concretely. If, for example, I wish to write the history of the nationalist movement in Egypt, in which the assassination of the Sirdar, Sir Lee Stack, is a dramatic moment, I must ascertain all the circumstances surrounding the tragedy. I should wish to interview every eye-witness of the attack and to compare the testimony of one with another. I would, of course, minutely examine the scene of the murder; take cognizance of the position of the Sirdar's motor-car; and calculate the position of the assassins. Nor could I consistently refrain from taking testimony from natives as well as from foreigners, from members of the Egyptian government as well as from British staff officers. The information brought together in this fashion would consist of testimony and circumstantial evidence—original material, from which I must, by painstaking analysis, construct my account of the deplorable affair. It need hardly be remarked that only an historian of so-called contemporary events would probably be in so favored a position that he could interrogate whom he pleased; but the illustration will serve its purpose if it makes clear that historical information is drawn from just such sources. But because so much of history is remote and because the actors and witnesses have passed away, testimony is usually not oral, but written, and circumstantial evidence must be wrested from mute objects, the remains of former human activities.

The broad distinction between records and remains is obvious. Records are documents designed to transmit information, in order either to perpetuate popular traditions and the memory of events, or to serve immediate practical purposes; while remains are mere inanimate vestiges of human life. Myths, folk-tales, ballads, and songs may be records, as well as anecdotes, genealogies, memoirs, biographies, paintings and works of art, annals, chronicles, and histories, though their value for historical purposes will vary greatly. Among records, too, must be included all those public and quasi-public documents which have a utilitarian purpose, such as proclamations, laws, treaties, ordinances, court records, legislative records, diplomatic papers, tax lists, maps and charts, charters, corporation records, canon laws, and ecclesiastical records of all sorts. And, finally, such private records as diaries, letters, commercial papers, wills, conveyances, and inventories, have an important place among historical sources. Remains, on the other hand, may include the tangible evidence of the ways of human society, such as sepulchres, temples, arms and armor, utensils, tools, clothing, adornments, weights and measures, coins, vehicles, houses, roads, bridges, and literature in general, as well as those intangible mental habits represented by language and its idioms, by names, and by proverbs, and those social institutions which are summed up in the terms worship, magic, marriage, and labor.

One kind of source material not included in this tabulation is oral tradition—the popular tales which are handed on from generation to generation by word of mouth without being committed to writing. As these are usually wonder-tales, they are of course liable to all the exaggeration which accompanies the repetition of a "good story." Under certain conditions, however, where the professional raconteur has a pride in keeping the conventional tradition intact, the tale may have a fixed content and a stereotyped form, and eventually may be set down in writing substantially unchanged. On these grounds the essential historicity of the Icelandic sagas is defended; but the details of even these sagas give rise to many doubts, and rarely do keepers-of-tradition resist the subtle temptation to enlarge and embellish a narrative.

The histories of Herodotus of Halicarnassus are vulnerable on this score. Writing at a time when men were wont to learn their history from the recital of epic poems, Herodotus carried over into prose many of the characteristics of the Homeric poets, such as the trick of digressing from the main narrative to tell an interesting story. Apropos of this characteristic, Dionysius of Halicarnassus, a literary critic in his day, remarks: "Herodotus knew that every narrative of great length wearies the ear of the hearer, if it dwells without a break on the same subject; but if pauses are introduced at intervals, it affects the mind agreeably. And so he desired to lend variety to his work and imitated Homer." Digressions and stories have their place in his narrative also because he wished to impress on the reader's mind the contrast of Hellenic with Oriental culture, which is indeed the keynote of his history, as Bury well points out.[1]

Yet when all this has been said, the fact remains that Herodotus had "a wonderful flair for a good story," which often betrayed him into an easy acceptance of improbable tales. One may picture this garrulous Ionian picking up bits of gossip and tradition in the streets of Memphis and repeating them as he heard them, saving his face where even his credulity could not reach by a cautious "They say but I do not vouch for it." And in the market-place at Athens, he doubtless

[1] J. B. Bury, *The Ancient Greek Historians*, pp. 42, 44.

heard the tales which Greek combatants in the Persian Wars told their children. Herodotus is by no means wholly uncritical; and at times he distinctly avoids committing himself on doubtful matters. "I am bound to state what is said," he remarks on one occasion, "but I am not bound to believe." "I do not disbelieve nor do I absolutely believe it," he says of an improbable tale.[1]

Herodotus drew also upon written sources. He alludes to Hecatæus of Miletus, the geographer, and borrows largely from the *Map of the World,* in which he described his travels in Egypt. Herodotus must have had access to Persian official documents, for he incorporates some of them in his text; and he makes frequent mention of monuments and works of art, such as the pyramids at Memphis, the bowl of Pausanias at Byzantium, and the boundary stone of Crœsus at Lydia.[2]

Thucydides offers a marked contrast to the "father of history." He had set himself a very different task. He purposed to write a history of the Peloponnesian War that should not be merely entertaining, but instructive. "The ac-

[1] *Ibid.*, p. 61.

[2] W. W. How and J. Wells, *A Commentary on Herodotus,* I, pp. 17 ff. See also the article on Herodotus by Jacoby in Paulys, *Real-Encyclopædie der classischen Altertumswissenschaft,* Supplement 1903.

curate knowledge of what has happened will be useful, because, according to human probability, similar things will happen again." He warns his readers against the songs of poets, whose profession it is to give all possible enlargements to their subjects, and against those writers of prose who study artful composition to catch the ear of the public. "As for the actions performed in the course of the war," he assures his readers, "I have not presumed to describe them from casual narratives or my own conjectures, but either from certainty, where I myself was a spectator, or from the most exact information I have been able to collect from others."

Nor can a modern historian who loves truth do less than this gifted Greek. Edward Freeman studied afoot all the battlefields of the Norman conquest of England, and based his narrative on his own topographical observations as well as on the testimony of contemporaries of the Conqueror. It is in his *History of the Norman Conquest* that we meet a unique sort of source material. Writing of the building of the fleet which was to carry William and his army across the Channel, Freeman says: "As soon as the undertaking was finally determined on, the woods of Normandy began to be felled and the havens of Normandy resounded with the axes and hammers of carpenters and shipbuilders." This is all plausible enough, but how did the historian know? In a footnote he refers his readers to Wace and "the tapestry." Now Wace was the author of a metrical chronicle of the Norman dukes and none too reliable a chronicler, Freeman to the contrary notwithstanding;[1] but the tapestry—the famous Bayeux Tapestry—is the pictorial story of the Conquest embroidered on a long linen roll by contemporary needlewomen. Freeman considers this record as "the highest authority on the Norman side . . . with hardly any of the inventions, exaggerations, and insinuations of the other Norman authorities. . . . In fact, the material has a certain advantage. Stitchwork must tell its tale simply and straightforward."

Those who wrote upon ancient history, in the eighteenth century, were restricted in their source material to the testimony of Greek and Roman historians, often of no great reliability. Since then thousands of inscriptions have been

[1] Freeman calls Wace an "honest and painstaking inquirer"; but J. H. Round holds that Wace, who wrote nearly a century after the Conquest, based his account on "a congeries of authorities." See *Feudal England*, p. 410; and also an article on "Historical Research" in *The Nineteenth Century*, vol. 44 (1898), in which Freeman's methods are roundly scored.

made available which have permitted an entire reconstruction of phases of ancient history. No one can take up a scholarly book on Roman history without being impressed by the weight of authority attached to these memorials carved on what was believed to be imperishable material. Even so simple a statement that the Emperor Hadrian had held certain petty offices at Rome rests upon the authority of an inscription found at Athens in the year 1862, in the course of excavations in the Theatre of Dionysius.[1]

It is a long leap from the Theatre of Dionysius to the plains of Kansas and the conflict over slavery in the American Republic, yet throughout this long span of time the essential nature of historical research has remained the same. When James Ford Rhodes undertook to narrate the bloody events in Kansas, he had to rely on such testimony as he could find in the printed pages of the report of the House Committee on Kansas, in the *Congressional Globe*, and in that unique modern institution, the daily newspaper. "I have examined or have had examined," writes Rhodes apropos of a single point, "the files of

[1] Bernard W. Henderson, *The Life and Principate of the Emperor Hadrian* (1923), p. 19.

the New York *Journal of Commerce*, the New York *Herald*, the Philadelphia *Pennsylvanian* . . . the Washington *Union*, and the Cleveland *Plain Dealer*."[1]

And Samuel Rawson Gardiner, after describing the dramatic attempt of King Charles I to seize the five members of the Commons, on the eve of the Civil War, in the tenth volume of his *History of England*, adds simply, "I have put my account together from the narratives in Rushworth, D'Ewes, and the Verney Notes."[2]

If these varied sources—traditions, metrical chronicles, tapestries, inscriptions, congressional reports, newspapers, narratives, journals, and diaries—were brought together and placed side by side, they would all appear as merely different kinds of testimony, testimony based on direct or indirect observation. When Thucydides affirms facts of his own knowledge, he is merely adding his testimony to that of others. Historical research must begin with testimony in some form as its main source of information.

The first task of every historian, if he would attempt original research, is to collect and col-

[1] James Ford Rhodes, *History of the United States from the Compromise of* 1850, II, p. 198.

[2] Samuel R. Gardiner, *History of England from the Accession of James I to the Outbreak of the Civil War*, 1603–1642, X, p. 140.

late his sources. And because of the ramifications of even the simplest theme, he can rarely dispense with the aid of the great storehouses of information—libraries, archives, and museums. The modern historian has immense advantages over his early predecessors, in possessing accessible libraries. Libraries existed even in remote antiquity, it is true: that of King Assurbanipal of Assyria at Nineveh dates from the seventh century before the Christian era. It was discovered by Layard in 1845, and its contents brought to London—not books in the modern sense, but clay tablets with cuneiform writing. The greatest library of classical antiquity was that founded by the Ptolemies at Alexandria. Public and private libraries multiplied in the late Roman Empire, particularly under the influence of religious orders. But the contents of these libraries, again, were not books, but manuscripts, for the book as the modern man knows it came into existence, of course, with the invention of printing from movable type.

Papyrus was the writing material *par excellence* of the ancient world. It was manufactured from a reed widely cultivated both in the delta of the Nile and in Sicily. Sheets of papyrus were pasted together, end to end, to form a roll; and the roll written on one side was the book of the ancient Latin and Greek world.[1] For reasons that are not altogether clear, perhaps because of a shortage of papyrus, the skins of sheep, goats, and kids gradually came into general use as writing material, and eventually supplanted papyrus. Known as parchment, or vellum, this new material was preferred by ecclesiastical writers because their bulky manuscripts could be used more conveniently when the leaves of vellum were strung together by thongs. Hence the term caudex, or codex, came into general use. For many centuries papyrus rolls, containing for the most part pagan literature, and parchment or vellum codices, containing the canonical scriptures and patristic writings, existed side by side, until vellum in turn gave way to the use of paper in the course of the fifteenth century.

Archives—depositaries of official records—were also known in ancient times. One purpose of the library of King Assurbanipal at Nineveh, indeed, was to serve as a storehouse for the safe-keeping of public records. Under the ruins of the royal palace at Tel-el-Amarna, in Egypt, were

[1] The Latins called it *liber* or *libellus;* the Greeks, *biblos* or *biblion.* The Latins spoke of a manuscript rolled up as *volumen,* but the Latinists of the Middle Ages used the term *rotulus.*

found in 1887 fragments of a hall of records and some three hundred clay tablets with inscriptions reaching back to the fifteenth century before the Christian era. The public documents of Rome were long preserved in the Temple of Saturn. During the Middle Ages, local archives were established when a religious house, a cathedral, a municipal or trading corporation felt the need of safeguarding its records. With the development of the papal office and the rise of modern states central archives were founded which now contain priceless secular and ecclesiastical documents. Among the most famous are the Vatican, the Archives Nationales at Paris, the Public Record Office at London, the Archivo General at Valladolid, and the Staatsarchive in Berlin and in Vienna.

Museums for the preservation of historical monuments and works of art are modern institutions. In ancient times, it is true, individuals collected objects of art for the gratification of their own tastes, and magistrates adorned public places with statues, fountains, and whatnot; but at best such collections were temporary. It was not until the revival of classical antiquity under the lead of the Italian humanists that public museums were founded to shelter the treasures of ancient art. France and England took the lead in the seventeenth century, but even in these countries the conception of the museum as a public institution took form slowly. The very term museum did not come into use until the following century; and general admission to museums was not granted until the close of the eighteenth century. The last century was the great age for the founding of museums. Collections of objects of art, ancient and modern, collections of inscriptions and coins, archæological and ethnographical museums, and picture galleries are now found in all the great cities of Europe and America.

Historical research has been greatly facilitated, too, by the collection and editing of records, either by private initiative or by the aid of societies. There is a type of scholar hardly known to the general public without whom the writing of history would be well-nigh impossible. It is he who has separated the chaff from the wheat in ancient and mediæval manuscripts, who has established correct texts, who has collected fugitive material, who has dated and located inscriptions and manuscripts, and who has collated and edited those great collections which are indispensable to the historian of ancient and mediæval times. A few titles will indicate the scope of these great collections. The *Corpus Inscriptionum Græcarum* and the *Corpus Inscriptionum Latinarum* contain inscriptions gathered from all parts of the Mediterranean world. Another collection, numbering over five hundred volumes, includes the texts of nearly all writers of classical antiquity and carries the title *Bibliotheca Scriptorum Græcorum et Romanorum Teubneriana.* Nearly all the larger states of Europe have undertaken to collect the writings of their early historians and annalists and their ancient laws and public records. Germany has its *Monumenta Germaniæ Historica;* England, its *Rerum Britannicarum Aevi Scriptores* and its *State Papers;* France, its *Collection de documents inédits sur l'histoire de France.*

Protracted intensive study of these manuscript sources has given birth to a numerous progeny of highly specialized arts, such as palæography, epigraphy, diplomatics, sphragistics, and heraldry. To the palæographer, a specialist in handwriting, the historian owes the use of many manuscripts which, unnamed, undated, and sometimes undeciphered, would have been closed codices. The study of epigraphy has made inscriptions available for historical purposes. And because the chanceries of Europe had different methods of drafting, signing, sealing, and attesting decrees, ordinances, charters, and other records, a fund of special knowledge had to be accumulated before scholars could identify and interpret these documents. The term diplomatics covers this highly important art; but diplomatists must often summon two other specialists to their aid—the student of seals and the expert in heraldry.

The results achieved by these laborious studies are often amazing. The German historian Giesebrecht, for example, pointed out that certain chronicles of the eleventh century drew their information from a common source which was no longer available. So sure was he of their dependence upon this early chronicle, which he named *Annales Altahenses*, that he constructed the missing manuscript from these later derivatives. Some twenty-six years later the missing chronicle was found, and it confirmed these shrewd conjectures in every important particular.

The studies of Professor George E. Woodbine on the manuscripts of Bracton exhibit American textual scholarship at its best.[1] It was imperative

[1] *Bracton de Legibus et Consuetudinibus Angliæ*, Edited by George E. Woodbine (1915–   ).

that the pedigrees of all the manuscript copies of Bracton's *De Legibus* should be ascertained before the editing of a reasonably correct text could be undertaken. The two volumes already published have set a high standard of scholarly excellence. Even in American historical research, constructive editing is sometimes necessary. One of the perplexing problems which baffled students of the Federal Convention of 1787 was the so-called plan for a new federal government drawn up by Charles Pinckney. The copy which Pinckney sent to John Quincy Adams in 1818, when Adams was preparing the *Journal* of the convention for publication, was clearly not the plan which he laid before that body. Yet Pinckney undoubtedly did draft a plan which he set before the convention. What was it? By a painstaking examination of the entries in the *Journal*, in Madison's notes, and in other sources, Doctor J. F. Jameson constructed what he conceived to be the actual plan which Pinckney proposed. What, then, was the draft which Pinckney, probably in good faith, sent to Adams? "Practically," concludes Doctor Jameson, "the so-called Pinckney plan consists of the report of the Committee of Detail, as brought in on August 6, minus some of its lesser features, and plus some of those of his real plan." Before this study was completed, its conclusions were strikingly corroborated by the discovery of a copy of Pinckney's real plan among the papers of James Wilson, a member of the convention from Pennsylvania.[1]

The rapid extension of historical information about the ancient world has been due to the activities of another group of specialists. It is to the spade of the archæologist that we owe the discovery of buried remains on the site of Troy, at Cnossus in Crete, in Mesopotamia, in Syria, in the Valley of the Nile, and throughout the peninsula of Italy.[2] Since the discovery of *De Bello Actiaco* at Herculaneum in 1752, more than ten thousand papyri have been brought to light, which contain not only copies of texts already known but hitherto unknown writings, ranging from fragments of apocryphal gospels and histories of early Christian martyrs to lists of victors in the Olympic games, Aristotle's *Constitution of Athens*, and fragments of Greek poetry.

[1] The detection of this plan is also a capital illustration of skilful critical analysis, for it was embedded, so to speak, without title, in a manuscript written by Wilson. This interesting analysis may be followed in Jameson's "Studies in the History of the Federal Convention of 1787," printed in the *Annual Report of the American Historical Association* for 1902, Vol. I.

[2] See Adolf Michaelis, *A Century of Archæological Discoveries* (1908).

And as I write comes the welcome news that the American School of Classical Studies at Athens has acquired a concession from the Greek government which will make possible a thorough exploration of the area to the north of the Acropolis, once the very heart of civic life.

History has this in common with the physical sciences that its content is steadily expanding. A chance discovery in a dump heap at Fayoum may necessitate an entire shift in our point of view or in our interpretation of events not only in Egyptian history but in that of the Mediterranean world. In his *History of the Peloponnesian War*, Thucydides remarks: "Minos is the earliest person whom we know from tradition to have been master of a navy, and to have been chiefly lord of the sea which is called the Grecian. To him the isles of Cyclades were subject; nay, most of them he himself planted with colonies." This tradition and the cycle of myths which centred in the person of this mysterious King of Crete had not been thought to have any sound basis in fact, until excavations were undertaken in 1900 which revealed unmistakable evidence that a great kingdom had flourished on the island of Crete between 1600 and 1100 B. C. Archæologists have since uncovered not only spacious palaces but works of art that bear witness to a high degree of culture, which spread to Asia Minor and the eastern coasts of the Mediterranean Sea, while remains of fortifications in the coastal towns seem to bear out the tradition, repeated by Thucydides, that the Cretan kingdom was a sea power of no mean proportions. And the twentieth century is likely to witness even more remarkable discoveries in the countries of the Mediterranean.

NOTE TO CHAPTER I

It is somewhat unfortunate that the word history should be used in several different senses. In its origin (Greek *ἱστορία*) it meant learning by inquiry. The historian (*ἱστορέων*) was a searcher after knowledge, an investigator. But by a subtle transformation the term came to be applied to the record or narrative of what had been learned by investigation; and in this sense it passed over into the Latin *historia* and into modern speech. So it was that well down into modern times history was conceived as a branch of literature or philosophy, rather than as a scientific inquiry. It was not until the beginning of the sixteenth century that attempts were made to give history an independent status. I have attempted to trace the evolution in a later chapter.

Meantime another ambiguity has caused confusion in thought. The word history is used to denote not only the record of what has been learned by inquiry, but also the course of events themselves. We speak of the *History of Rome*, meaning that written by Livy, Mommsen, Ferrero;

but also we speak of Roman history as a series of happenings in time and space, as if it existed apart from records. This ambiguity often results in the unconscious assumption that the past of humanity has a sort of objective reality with which, in some unexplained way, the historical scholar may compare and verify the written records. It need hardly be reiterated that we can know the past only as it has left its traces in records and remains. The past does not exist except in human consciousness.

In this connection, too, it may be observed that the periods of history are an artificial creation. There is no ancient, mediæval, and modern history except as historians thus divide the record of humanity into compartments; and it is a fair question whether this periodization has not hindered rather than helped the cause of learning, by creating arbitrary divisions which have insidiously obscured the essential continuity of the evolution of human society. And, finally, the assumed distinction between contemporary history and past history breaks down in the face of the obvious inability of the human mind to hold the fleeting moment.[1] That which I call the present is already past. It differs from all that passed through my mind long ago only by reason of the freshness of memory which gives it a deceptive immediateness. The present which we would hold has slipped into the limbo of the past and can only be reclaimed, as all human experience is recovered, through the traces which it has left.

Even if, as the exponents of the new history somewhat querulously demand, history should abandon its traditional function of telling what has been or how it came to be, and become a science of human evolution advancing from the particular to the universal, the need of a fact-finding and fact-attesting discipline would still be as great as ever.

[1] B. Croce, *History: Its Theory and Practice*, ch. 1.

For it is, in part at least, by virtue of the data furnished by historical research that the social sciences make their generalizations. To kick away the ladder by which these newer studies have mounted, is to assume altogether too rashly that the social sciences have reached an eminence from which they no longer need to survey the past, and that historical scholars have exhausted their sources of information.

Whatever history may or may not include—much ink has been spilled over the question—no one is likely to mistake the significance of the word *historical*. It indicates a point of view, a way of describing things, a method of approach to the study of phenomena. "The older historians" may describe the march of political events that ended in the rise of a new national state; "the new historians" may account for a popular movement by stressing the economic and geographical conditions which produced it; sociologists may undertake to explain social institutions in the light of their origin; biographers may try to account for behavior by searching for early repressions and concealed complexes; newspaper reporters may write up the story of crime or of a public catastrophe—in each and every case, the facts, the phenomena, the events, must be viewed as a succession in time. And so long as this historical point of view is maintained, it does not much matter whether the study be called history or sociology, old history or new history, biography or psychoanalysis, ancient history or current events, or simply news.

CHAPTER II

THE BASIS OF HISTORICAL DOUBT

On the sixteenth of September, 1920, a mysterious bomb explosion occurred on Wall Street, in New York City, exactly at noon, when ordinarily the street would have been crowded with people and vehicles. That many casualties did not occur seems little short of miraculous. The perpetrators of the outrage and their motive are still unknown. The editor of *The Wall Street Journal*, who was near the scene of the explosion, at once sent out reporters to "cover the matter" and himself interrogated some nine "eye-witnesses." Eight of these testified that there were a number of vehicles in the block: some said as many as ten; and three testified positively that a red motor-truck carried the bomb. Only one, a retired army officer, testified that the explosion occurred upon a small horse-drawn truck standing opposite the entrance of the Assay Office, and that the only other vehicle in sight was a motorcar on the opposite side; and his testimony was proved correct. "It should be noted," adds the editor, "that this was an expert witness. As a military man he was acquainted with the nature of explosives and he had been trained to observe correctly. Every one of the remaining eight witnesses was wrong on the important question of the vehicles in the block. . . . Eight of them told not what they had seen but what they had inferred, and even what they had guessed. . . . Speaking as a newspaper observer of thirty-five years' experience all over the world, accustomed to gather news and therefore to weigh evidence, it seems to me we are all more or less unconscious liars." [1]

Since so much of history rests upon just such contemporary testimony, no historian can afford to neglect the general psychological conditions governing observation. In recent years experimental psychologists have put at his disposal a very considerable fund of information relating to perception, by which he might profit if he would. It is rather extraordinary that while the best treatise on the principles of legal evidence[2] gives a large place to these empirical facts, no treatise on historical method has applied them

[1] Letter to *The New York Times*, May 30, 1924.

[2] *The Principles of Judicial Proof as Given by Logic, Psychology, and General Experience, and Illustrated in Judicial Trials;* compiled by John Henry Wigmore (1913).

to its peculiar problems. Far too much stress has been laid on the honesty or candor of historical witnesses and far too little upon their probable apperceptive powers and the conditions under which they exercised them.

Nothing could seem more obvious than that human beings see with their eyes and hear with their ears. It is hard to convince the unlettered man that the process of perception is not direct and simple. "Seeing is believing" is an old adage. Yet psychology teaches that the process of perception is highly complex. Undoubtedly knowledge begins with sensory impressions—with stimulation of the sensory organs; but these sensory stimuli do not primarily produce sight and hearing, but rather the raw material for such perceptions. Experiments indicate that, so far as the individual can isolate his sensations in consciousness, he is aware of diffused qualities, such as brightness and color, noises and tones. Ordinarily, however, these vague sensory impressions are differentiated immediately by the activity of attention, and objectified. This is the process of perception. "Sensation, as giving the qualitative determinant to all sensory experience, is not only the first stage in the perceptual process, furnishing the vague undifferentiated matrix out of which the richness of qualitative variety is later extradited by analysis, but it is also the constant accompaniment of sensory activities, giving the stuff, the material, out of which perception is elaborated." [1]

It seems to be the peculiarity of perception, so far as that process can be isolated in consciousness, that it involves awareness of objects rather than of qualities. It has been defined, indeed, as "the consciousness of particular material things present to sense." Now a chair has peculiar qualities and parts—arms, legs, back, seat, but we do not see the four legs, two arms, back, and seat, and put them together as a chair: we perceive the chair as a single whole. Doubtless many sensory nerves have been stimulated, but we perceive a single unified object. How can this be? Only because perception consists in bringing earlier experience to bear upon the new content in consciousness. Other perceptions have taught the characteristics of chairs and have produced habitual reactions. "We come . . . upon this striking fact, that in some manner or other, perception involves a rudimentary *reproductive* pro-

[1] James R. Angell, *Psychology: an Introductory Study of the Structure and Function of Human Consciousness*, p. 121.

cess. Somehow, our former perceptions are taken up and incorporated into our present perceptions, modifying them and moulding them into accord with the past."[1] The perceived object is not merely the vibrations set up in our sensory end-organs, like the retina of the eye, but these impulses integrated and interpreted by past experience. "Every time we open our eyes to see, or our ears to hear, what *we can* see and hear in a true sense and a large measure is determined for us by what we have *previously learned* to see and hear."[2]

Illusions illustrate the process of perception. We speak of an illusion as a deception of the senses, but the fault is not with the sense organs. Ordinarily, in a healthy person, they perform their proper functions. When we misread a printed word, the image on the retina has not played us false. We have read into the image something that is not there or we have omitted what is present, because of some train of association or of some suggested idea. Laboratory tests have demonstrated the power of suggestion.

A very familiar instance of this process is the constant overlooking of misprints—false letters,

[1] *Ibid.*, p. 125.

[2] *Ibid.*, p. 139.

transposed letters, and missing letters—unless these happen to be particularly striking. We see only the general physiognomy of the word, and the detailed features are supplied from within; in this case it is the expected that happens. In a series of experiments by Professor Münsterberg a word was briefly shown, while just before a certain idea or train of thought was suggested. Under these circumstances the word shown was often misread in accordance with the suggested idea; if the idea of future is suggested, part may be read as past; if vegetable is the suggested line of thought, fright may be read as fruit, and so on. Reading is thus done largely by the mental eye; and entire words, obviously suggested by the context, are sometimes read in, when they have been accidentally omitted.[1]

The success of conjuring tricks depends very largely upon the ability of the conjurer to misdirect attention by suggestion.

He looks intently at his extended right hand, involuntarily carrying our eyes to the same spot while he is doing the trick with the unobserved left hand. . . . A call upon the attention in one direction prevents its dispersion in another. . . . Houdini gives it as one of his rules never to announce beforehand the nature of the effect which you intend to produce, in order that the specta-

[1] Joseph Jastrow, *Fact and Fable in Psychology*, pp. 279–280.

tor may not know where to fix his attention. He also tells us that whenever you count "*one, two, three,*" as preliminary to the disappearance of an object, the real vanishing must take place before you say "*three*"—for the audience have their attention fixed upon "*three,*" and whatever is done at "one" or "two" entirely escapes their notice. The "patter" or setting of a trick often constitutes the real art of its execution, because it directs or rather misdirects the attention.[1]

The relative slowness of human vision has important consequences. The moving-picture camera shows that the eye does not perceive the successive rapid movements of a galloping horse, for example, but constructs an image of a galloping horse by grouping or compounding a number of sense impressions into a so-called instantaneous representation.[2] In much the same way quite unconsciously an observer will fill in the gaps in his vision by interpolating objects according to his expectations. Some years ago I was obliged for a time to lecture in a college building the upper rooms of which were used by medical students for dissection. The odors wafted downstairs were exceedingly disagreeable; and more than once the remains of the dis-

[1] Joseph Jastrow, *Fact and Fable in Psychology,* pp. 120–121.
[2] Hans Gross, *Criminal Psychology* (1911) p. 198.

secting room were carried uncovered through the hall with shocking carelessness. One morning, on approaching the building with a colleague, I expressed my general dissatisfaction with the arrangement in no uncertain words. As I threw open the door of the hall and sniffed the foul air my eyes caught sight of a human vertebra on the floor. "There!" said I in utter disgust. "Now you see what I have to put up with!" My colleague laughed and kicked the offensive thing lightly away. It was an *oak leaf* blown in through the open door!

The tendency of the mind to fill in the gaps of sense impressions is a highly significant fact for the historian. For what the mind adds is drawn either from its own individual experience or from the experience which it shares with a social group. A person of nervous temperament is quite likely to be affected in his reactions by the atmosphere of the group of which he is a member. He succumbs more readily to deceptions if those about him are susceptible. It is hard for such a person in a sympathetic group in a séance not to see what all desire to see—from ectoplasm to table-tipping. "Psychic contagion," "mental induction," "psychology of the crowd," are some of the phrases devised to explain the fact.

The peculiarities of vision are too numerous for detailed description in these pages, but two have a special interest for historical scholars. The first relates to estimates of size and distance. Münsterberg, copying an experiment already made by the astronomer Förster, asked a class of students to compare the apparent size of the full moon to that of some object held in the hand at arm's length.

"My list of answers," he reports, "begins as follows: quarter of a dollar; fair-sized canteloupe; at the horizon, large dinner-plate, overhead, dessert-plate; my watch; six inches in diameter; silver dollar; hundred times as large as my watch; man's head; fifty-cent piece; nine inches in diameter; grapefruit; carriage-wheel; butter-plate; orange; ten feet; two inches; one-cent piece; school-room clock; a pea; soup-plate; fountain pen; lemon pie; palm of the hand; three feet in diameter: enough to show, again, the overwhelming manifoldness of the impressions received. To the surprise of my readers, perhaps, it may be added at once that the only man who was right was the one who compared it to a pea."[1]

These results shatter confidence in casual testimony as to the size of isolated objects. And

[1] Hugo Münsterberg, *On the Witness Stand*, pp. 27–28.

as for estimates of distance, few observers bear in mind that not clearness alone but illumination must be taken into account. Distinctness of a perceptual image is usually made the criterion of distance. Hence objects seen dimly near at hand in a fog are magnified and seem far away, while objects seen clearly in the atmosphere of mountainous regions seem smaller and near at hand. Illumination also affects perception of color. It is now well known that at night, with the decrease of illumination, red disappears before blue. If then a witness should testify in court that he had seen a red cap at dusk but not a blue coat, his testimony would be discounted at once.[1]

Differences in the sense of hearing are too well understood to need emphasis. Less familiar are peculiarities in the perception of the direction of sound. Successive experiments have demonstrated that loud sounds are usually located in front of the hearer, and that sounds to his right or left are most easily distinguished by him. These facts may explain a number of historical puzzles, as, for example, the conflict of testimony as to what Martin Luther really said at the Diet of Worms.

[1] Hans Gross, *Criminal Psychology* (1911), p. 206.

Perceptions of time are notoriously deceptive. It has been pointed out that we are never conscious of a mere point of time, but rather of extent and duration. "Consciousness of time is proportional to our interest and absorption in the occupation of the moment." Every one knows from his own experience how time drags on a disagreeable journey and how swiftly the moments fly when a well-acted drama holds our attention. Yet, oddly enough, in recollection these long disagreeable periods seem very short, while the happy moments acquire greater duration. The apparent paradox has been explained as follows: "Our feeling for the length of these remembered intervals depends upon the amount of content, the number of events, which we can read back into them. The interesting intervals are full of such things, whereas the tedious periods are characterized by a depressing sameness, which affords our memory little or nothing to lay hold upon." [1]

It need hardly be said that if the original perception of historical events be imperfect or faulty, the testimony of even an honest and candid observer can have little evidential value. It is less obvious that the testimonial process

[1] J. R. Angell, *Psychology*, pp. 158–159.

itself has peculiarities which may be studied profitably from the viewpoint of psychology. Münsterberg gives the following account of an experiment made by Professor Liszt at Berlin many years ago:

The professor had spoken about a book. One of the older students suddenly shouts, "I want to throw light on the matter from the standpoint of Christian morality!" Another student throws in, "I cannot stand that!" The first starts up exclaiming, "You have insulted me!" The second clenches his fist and cries, "If you say another word—" The first draws a revolver. The second rushes madly upon him. The professor steps between them and, as he grasps the man's arm, the revolver goes off. General uproar. In that moment Professor Liszt secures order and asks a part of the students to write an exact account of all that has happened. The whole had been a comedy, carefully planned and rehearsed by the three actors for the purpose of studying the exactitude of observation and recollection. Those who did not write the report at once were, part of them, asked to write it the next day or a week later; and others had to depose their observations under cross-examination. The whole objective performance was cut up into fourteen little parts which referred partly to actions, partly to words. As mistakes there were counted the omissions, the wrong additions, and the alterations. The smallest number of mistakes gave twenty-six per cent of erroneous statements; the largest was eighty per cent. The reports with reference to the second half of the performance, which was more strongly emotional, gave an average of fifteen per cent more mistakes than those of the first half. Words were put into the mouths of men who had been silent spectators during the whole short episode; actions were attributed to the chief participants of which not the slightest trace existed; and essential parts of the tragi-comedy were completely eliminated from the memory of a number of witnesses.[1]

A similar experiment at a meeting of a scientific association in Göttingen yielded even more extraordinary results, for in this instance the jurists, psychologists, and physicians present were men trained in habits of scientific observation. In their reports of an artfully planned episode which interrupted one of the meetings, more than half of these scientific men omitted or falsified fifty per cent of the happenings which occurred directly before them.[2]

[1] Hugo Münsterberg, *On the Witness Stand*, pp. 49–51.

[2] Important experiments and studies in the psychology of testimony have been made by German psychologists, but their findings have not been made accessible in translation, except for a short abstract of lectures by W. Stern in *The American Journal of Psychology* for April, 1910. See L. W. Stern, *Die Psychologie der Aussage* (1902); O. Lippman, *Grundriss der Psychologie für Juristen* (1908); J. Schrenk, *Einführung in die Psychologie der Aussage* (1922).

The errors in these instances were not due merely to what is commonly termed a faulty memory. Each reported what he *thought* he saw and heard. For some reason or other the testimonial accounts deviated from the actual occurrences. Deflecting influences were at work. What were they? John Dewey makes an important contribution to the whole problem of the testimonial process when he says: "The revivals of memory are rarely literal. We naturally remember what interests us and because it interests us. . . . The primary life of memory is emotional rather than intellectual and practical." And again, "The primitive life of memory is one of fancy and imagination, rather than of accurate recollection."[1] Memory is therefore selective and discriminative, choosing out of the welter of past experience those moments which have an emotional value. In telling a story of personal experience, we inevitably select the details that interested us and we recount them with a distribution of emphasis which corresponds to our interests. And in an occurrence where the emotions are aroused, the deviations of memory will be more strongly marked, as in the case of the Göttingen scientists just described.

[1] John Dewey, *Reconstruction in Philosophy*, pp. 2–3.

Another consideration must be given weight. In every individual lurks the artist. The most prosaic of men have a certain amount of productive imagination, which makes them more or less dramatic in telling a story or in giving testimony. We are all subtly conscious of our audience. It is probably true, as John Dewey remarks, that "savage man recalled yesterday's struggle with an animal not in order to study in a scientific way the qualities of the animal or for the sake of calculating better how to fight to-morrow; but to escape from the tedium of to-day by regaining the thrill of yesterday. . . . Memory is vicarious experience in which there is all the emotional value of actual experience without its strains, vicissitudes, and troubles. . . . At the time of practical experience man exists from moment to moment preoccupied with the task of the moment. As he resurveys all the moments in thought, a drama emerges with a beginning, a middle, and a movement toward the climax of achievement or defeat."

After a lapse of time, the most candid narrator of events is often tricked into interpolation of details by fancy, by suggestion, by emotion, or by those subtle impressions which seem to lie just below the threshold of consciousness. Every one will find in his own experience ample corroboration of the vagaries of memory. No less a personage than the gifted historian, James Anthony Froude, was often the prey of just such deflecting influences, though Mr. Herbert A. L. Fisher declares that he was "constitutionally inaccurate," citing the following instances:

Writing . . . of Adelaide, in Australia, he [Froude] says: "Seven miles away we saw below us, in a basin with a river winding through it, a city of 150,000 inhabitants, not one of whom has ever known, or will ever know, one moment's anxiety as to the recurring regularity of his three meals a day." Adelaide is on high ground, not in a valley; there is no river running through it; its population was not more than 75,000; and, at the very moment when Mr. Froude visited it, a large portion of that population was on the verge of starvation. His fascinating book on the West Indies abounds with similar mistakes. Of Port of Spain, in Trinidad, he writes: "The streets are broad, and are planted with trees for shade; each house, where room permits, having a garden of its own with coffee-plants. There is abundance of rain, and the gutters which run down by the footway are flushed almost every day." As a matter of fact, the streets are narrow; they are not planted with trees; very few of the houses have gardens; and I have been assured by a resident that he has never heard of a garden being planted with the coffee-plant. The gutters are indeed flushed with sufficient frequency during the rainy season, which lasts five months; but Mr. Froude was in Trinidad during the latter part of January, in the height of the dry season, when a heavy fall of rain is quite exceptional.[1]

The defects of memory are only too well known. Misdating of details in a complicated story is a common error. A typical instance is John Adams's account of the drafting of the Declaration of Independence. Adams was then eighty-eight years old, and forty-seven years had elapsed since the events of June, 1776. After reciting the circumstances which led to the appointment of a committee of independence by Congress, Adams writes:

The committee had several meetings, in which were proposed the articles of which the Declaration was to consist, and minutes made of them. The committee then appointed Mr. Jefferson and me to draw them up in form, and clothe them in a proper dress.

The sub-committee met. Jefferson proposed to me to make the draft. I said, "I will not." "You should do it." "Oh! no." "Why will you

[1] "Modern Historians and their Methods," in *The Fortnightly Review*, December, 1894, p. 815.

not? You ought to do it." "I will not." "Why?" "Reasons enough." "What can be your reasons?" "Reason first—You are a Virginian, and a Virginian ought to appear at the head of this business. Reason second—I am obnoxious, suspected, and unpopular. You are very much otherwise. Reason third—You can write ten times better than I can." "Well," said Jefferson, "if you are decided, I will do as well as I can." "Very well. When you have drawn it up, we will have a meeting."

He accordingly took the minutes, and in a day or two produced to me his draft. Whether I made or suggested any correction, I remember not. The report was made to the committee of five, by them examined, but whether altered or corrected in any thing, I cannot recollect. But, in substance at least, it was reported to Congress, where, after a severe criticism, and striking out several of the most oratorical paragraphs, it was adopted on the fourth of July, 1776, and published to the world.[1]

Jefferson gives a different account, holding that Adams's memory had "led him into unquestionable error":

The committee of five met, no such thing as a sub-committee was proposed, but they unanimously pressed on myself alone to undertake

[1] *The Life and Works of John Adams*, vol. II, pp. 512–515.

the draft. I consented; I drew it; but before I reported it to the committee I communicated it separately to Doctor Franklin and Mr. Adams requesting their corrections; . . . and you have seen the original paper now in my hands, with the corrections of Doctor Franklin and Mr. Adams interlined in their own handwriting. Their alterations were two or three only, and merely verbal. I then wrote a fair copy, reported it to the committee, and from them, unaltered to the Congress.[1]

But Jefferson's own memory may have played him false in certain particulars. Certainly if he meant to imply that his "original paper" contained only the few corrections of Adams and Franklin, he has misstated the facts, for it contains many alterations not in their handwriting. And the "fair copy" which he wrote and reported to the committee has never been found.[2]

No one can read far in the literature of psychology without acquiring a wholesome scepticism respecting the alleged facts of history. Faced by the obvious fallibility of perception and memory in the best of witnesses, the serious student is disposed to wonder if Fontenelle was

[1] *Writings of Thomas Jefferson* (ed. 1869), vol. VII, p. 304.
[2] Becker, *The Declaration of Independence*, pp. 136–141.

not right, after all, when he remarked that history is a fable that men have agreed upon.[1] But unfortunately there is a great deal of history upon which men are not agreed. Nor have we even yet sounded the depths of the initial problem in all historical research.

There is a certain fallacy in depicting the historian as a sort of juror sitting in the court of history and weighing evidence. The word "testimony," which has appeared so frequently in these pages, is itself misleading. The implied analogy is imperfect. It is within the power of a modern court of justice to call witnesses to the stand; to observe them or to have them put under observation by experts of one sort or another; to cross-examine them; to put them under oath to tell the truth, the whole truth, and nothing but the truth. The historian can command none of these resources. For the most part, he must read such testimony as he has; rarely, except in the case of contemporary events, can he listen to or record the testimony of living witnesses. Would that he could call his witnesses to

[1] Justin Winsor fell a victim to this despondency in an article on "The Perils of Historical Narrative" in *The Atlantic Monthly*, vol. 66 (1890). "Historical accuracy is, in fact," he remarks, "the most fleeting of vanities. . . . No historical statement can be final. . . . It is this uncertainty that keeps historical study perennial."

the bar, scan their countenances, observe their reactions under cross-examination, awe them into truthfulness by administering oaths! Then, indeed, he might unlock the mysteries of the ages.

In still another respect, the historian is at a disadvantage. He cannot usually pick his witnesses. He must take whatever testimony is tossed up like flotsam and jetsam on the sea of time. He must stand helpless before many complicated happenings because chance has destroyed the testimony of important witnesses. In moments of despondency he is moved to believe that the fragments of testimony which have been wafted to him by the winds of chance have survived only because they are so light and trivial. And the attitude of modern criminologists toward certain kinds of testimony only intensifies his despondency. "Lack of conscientiousness," writes Gross, "is most characteristically frequent and sharply defined among people who have no real business in life. . . . The most hateful and the most dangerous of these people are the congenital tramps—people who did not have to work and faithfully pursued the opportunity of doing nothing. . . . Among the few rules without exception which in the course of long experience the criminologist may make, this is one—that *the real tramps of both sexes and all walks of life will never testify conscientiously.*" [1] How many of the often-quoted authorities in history, one wonders, were congenital tramps!

All attempts to range history beside the so-called natural sciences on an assumed identity of method must break down. The method that gives relative exactitude to physics and chemistry, for example, is that of trial and error. Successive observations of phenomena which can be made to recur at the will of the experimenter diminish the likelihood of error. Results obtained at one time and place, moreover, may be tested at other times and places by other observers. An experimental scientist is always keenly aware that his fellow workers are watching and testing his work. This consciousness is at once his protection and his inspiration. It holds him to scrupulous exactness in his processes and it assures him of recognition when he has solved his problem. Pasteur triumphed in his long struggles with the opponents of his germ theory when he demonstrated before his colleagues in the Académie de Médecine the presence of the *bacillus anthracis* in three hens each

[1] Hans Gross, *Criminal Psychology* (translated 1911), pp. 17–18.

of which had been subjected to inoculation under different conditions carefully noted.[1]

Then again, the actual happenings of human history never repeat themselves—the old adage to the contrary notwithstanding. The historical scholar can never resort to test tubes, culture mediums, and microscopes to test his hypotheses. The ongoings of human history constitute a unique series. No one can summon Luther before another Diet of Worms. Other fiery reformers there will be; but no Martin Luther; other diets, but none over which Charles the Fifth can be made to preside. That there may be a scientific study of human types and of societal institutions, need not be denied. The ways of reformers and the features of religious revolutions may become the subject of useful treatises. But the concrete events from which general deductions are made must ever remain unique.

The discrepancy between history and natural science widens when one considers the standing of the historical witness in the one case, and the position of the scientific observer in the other. No skilled physicist or chemist would wittingly

[1] René Vallery-Radot, *The Life of Pasteur* (translated by Mrs. R. L. Devonshire), 1919, pp. 267 ff.

leave his experiment in the hands of an untrained observer. He chooses his assistants with the same care that he gives to his apparatus. But the historian must take whom and what the gods vouchsafe. The chief witness to certain historical events may be an ignorant yokel or even a thoroughly unreliable character whose partisanship is a matter of notoriety. It not infrequently happens that an historical scholar finds himself in precisely the predicament of a physicist who should be called away from his experiment and have to trust to the casual observations of an ignorant and unskilled caretaker of the laboratory. But again the analogy fails, for the physicist can usually repeat the interrupted test.

Faith in the verity of history is shaken still further by another disturbing consideration. Who shall vouch for the truthfulness of an historical witness? In every-day life there are many ways of ascertaining the veracity of an informant. Within the circle of his acquaintances, every one knows intuitively those who habitually strive to state facts without exaggeration or understatement, and those who live in a world of their own creating and always view life through the deflecting prism of their emotions.

Every successful advocate knows how to discriminate between those who will make reliable witnesses and those who will not. The historian, however, is at a signal disadvantage in making such discriminations, because he must often make appraisal of the witness's honesty of purpose by scrutinizing a single utterance.

There remains a vital matter which historians have not considered with sufficient care. Given the testimony of a single witness whose general veracity is accepted and who was near enough to the events described, so that of him it may be said that he could have either seen or heard them, does such testimony establish the historical reality of the facts as narrated? It is astonishing to find how much history has been written on the supposition that such testimony has complete probative value. Yet even a modern court of law, with all legal resources at its command, hesitates to convict a prisoner at the bar on the single unsupported testimony of a witness. The tendency of legal procedure is to give less and less weight to the probative value of testimony and more and more to realistic or circumstantial proofs. "It must be admitted," writes a high authority on criminal psychology, "that at the present day the value of the testimony of even a truthful witness is much overrated. The numberless errors in perceptions derived from the senses, the faults of memory, the far-reaching differences in human beings as regards sex, nature, culture, mood of the moment, health, passionate excitement, environment—all these things have so great an effect that we scarcely ever receive two *quite similar* accounts of one thing; and between what people really experience and what they confidently assert, we find only error heaped upon error. Out of the mouths of two witnesses we *may* arrive at the real truth, we may form for ourselves an idea of the circumstances of an occurrence and satisfy ourselves concerning it, but the evidence will seldom be true and material; and whoever goes more closely into the matter will not silence his conscience, even after listening to ten witnesses. . . . As the science of criminal investigation proceeds, oral testimony falls behind and the importance of realistic proof advances; 'circumstances cannot lie,' witnesses can and do." [1]

[1] Hans Gross, *Criminal Investigation* (1907), Introduction, p. xxv.

CHAPTER III

THE TECHNIQUE OF HISTORICAL CRITICISM

In historical studies doubt is the beginning of wisdom. Unless one shakes off the credulity of the natural man and the disposition to follow authority—especially the authority of the written or printed word—he can never attain new and independent points of view in history. It is only by resolutely questioning the authenticity and value of sources that a mastery of historical facts can be won. In no field of scholarship does the dead hand of tradition weigh more heavily, for human emotions and passions are often involved in the preservation of this or that interpretation of history. Nearly all the mediæval chroniclers were propagandists, and even some modern historians have consciously or unconsciously become the defenders of a faith or a sect, a principle or a party.

Detailed examination of source material must precede an evaluation of its worth. For unless a mediæval manuscript, for example, can be dated and assigned to some locality as its place of origin, and the standing of its author discovered, it is of little value for historical purposes. It may not be at all what it seems to be; its author may have no direct knowledge of the events he describes; it may even be fabricated. The appraisal of any historical material involves, first of all, determination of the time when it was fabricated, written, or printed, and of the place where it originated; then, the more difficult determination of its authorship. This is the process usually described as external criticism.[1] If accurately and painstakingly done, it should decide once for all whether or no the historical material is genuine and may be used further as circumstantial or testimonial evidence; and, if genuine, whether it is a primary or a secondary source.

Generally speaking an undated document is worthless for historical purposes. Sometimes it will suffice to know that a document belongs to one epoch or another, where its importance consists in its outward form, as an example of writing or printing, or of court practice, or of

[1] "Die äussere Kritik," says Bernheim, "beurteilt die Tatsächlichkeit des Quellenmaterials, d. h. ob die einzelnen Quellen überhaupt als historische Zeugnisse zuzulassen sind, bezw. inwieweit, und sie richtet die so gesichteten Quellen zu weiterer Benutzung her." E. Bernheim, *Lehrbuch der Historischen Methode* (Sechste Auflage, 1908), p. 330.

administrative procedure. Usually, however, it is highly important to assign a more precise date, if its contents are to be used as testimony to historical events. Particularly, mediæval public documents, which often lack dates because of the carelessness or indifference of copyists, must be dated if their contents are to shed light on a chain of events. So, too, undated letters in the correspondence of a Cavour, a Bismarck, and a Palmerston must be dated to serve the purpose of a biographer.

Most mediævalists, with their technical training in palæography and philology, can readily assign an undated document to a definite period because of peculiarities of handwriting, language, and style. For more precise dating, significant allusions or phrases must be sought out in the document. An allusion to some well-known occurrence—an eclipse, an earthquake, a riot, an election—may point to an approximate date. Not infrequently a chance reference to another point of time will lead to a precise dating of the document. The date of the interesting pamphlet entitled *Strange News from Virginia*—to take a later instance—can be fixed almost exactly by casual allusions to well-known facts such as the death of Nathaniel Bacon, and by such expressions as "the 25th of June last," "last summer," "in which lamentable condition that unhappy Continent has remained for the space of almost a twelvemonth." The account must have been written before the end of June 1677, and after the news of Bacon's death reached England.[1]

When other precise means fail, a document may be given an approximate date by ascertaining the earliest and the latest points of time when it could have been written. Between these limits—somewhat pedantically termed *terminus post quem* and *terminus ante quem*—the document may be placed. The closer the limits, the more exact the dating. An excellent example of this method is the dating of the *Annales Laurissenses,* a chronicle of the time of Charlemagne, which records the events of the period 741–829. A *terminus post quem* is given first by an entry for the year 772: *et inde perrexit* [*i. e.*, domnus Carolus—Charlemagne] *partibus Saxoniæ prima vice.* It is a fair inference that the chronicler would not have said "for the first time" (*prima vice*) if he had not known of the second expedition to Saxony, which took place in 775. At least, the chronicle must have been written after that

[1] The account was published in London in 1677.

date. But further reading reveals a later date. For the year 777 there is this entry: *tunc domnus Carolus rex sinodum publicum habuit ad Paderbrunnen prima vice.* Again the betraying phrase. Evidently the author knew of a second diet at Paderborn. This we know met in 785, which at once displaces the earlier date. The *terminus post quem* is now the year 785. Once again: in the year 781 the chronicle, alluding to Count Tassilo of Bavaria, reads: *sed non diu promissiones quas fecerat conservavit.* Beyond a doubt, the author knew of the Count's fall from grace in the year 788. The chronicle must have been written after this date. Here then is the *terminus post quem.*

There is only a single indication of the *terminus ante quem.* For the year 785 the chronicle has this item: *et tunc tota Saxonia subjugata est.* This the author would hardly have said if he had known of the uprising of all Saxony in 793. Sometime before this date, then, the chronicle must have been written. This skilful narrowing of the limits leaves scarcely any doubt that the *Annales Laurissenses* were written between 788 and 793.[1]

This method may be used with equal success

[1] Bernheim, *Lehrbuch,* pp. 397–8.

in the somewhat rare cases where modern documents have to be dated. A brilliant, though not highly important, piece of critical scholarship was the dating of Bancroft's *Life of Martin Van Buren* by the late Professor Edward Bourne. The biography was published in 1889 but unquestionably written years before. Bourne noted the absence of any statement of Van Buren's views on the vexed Texas question in 1844 and concluded that the biographer could not have known Van Buren's attitude, which was first announced in a letter written April 20, 1844, and at once published by the press. The book must then have been written before the publication of this letter in the newspapers (April 27) and probably before April 20, 1844. So important a matter would not have been passed over deliberately by the biographer. The earliest date is fixed by the allusion to Van Buren's letter of June 19, 1843, expressing sympathy for Ireland, though possibly Bancroft would not have felt free to use this letter, had it not appeared in print. The letter appeared in *Niles' Register* under date of October 7, 1843. Bourne concluded, therefore, that Bancroft had written the biography in the expectation that Van Buren would be nominated for the presidency in 1844. When, therefore, the unexpected happened, and Polk was nominated by the Democratic Convention, this campaign biography was laid aside. This conclusion received a striking confirmation in letters of Bancroft to Van Buren, first printed in 1909 in the *Proceedings* of the Massachusetts Historical Society.[1]

A printed book or pamphlet rarely fails to bear the outward and visible mark of its origin. There is usually little difficulty in finding where it was printed. But there may be great difficulty in ascertaining where it was composed, for when a strict censorship of the press is maintained, authors may send manuscripts to foreign countries to be printed. Works were printed in Holland and Geneva in the Age of the Puritan Revolution which would have sent the authors to the pillory in England. It may be a matter of considerable moment to find out where and under what circumstances a mediæval manuscript originated. Outward characteristics, such as handwriting, language, dialect, and style, may furnish some clues to the birthplace of a manuscript; and a mediævalist may unhesitatingly place some manuscripts by reason of idiomatic

[1] See the communication of Professor Max Farrand in *The American Historical Review*, vol. 17, pp. 680–681.

peculiarities. The contents can hardly fail to betray interest in or familiarity with happenings in certain regions. The annals found in the Cloister of Saint Michael's at Lüneburg were finally traced back to their place of origin by means of the recurring allusions to the affairs of the Counts of Saxony and to the history of the monastery of Rosenfeld, which they founded. The author repeatedly assumes that his readers are familiar with these undistinguished Saxon princes, even to the extent of knowing the nick-names which they bear and with the trivial hap-penings within the walls of Rosenfeld. A brief record for the year 1130 reads "*Cono abbas obiit,*" assuming that the reader must know this Cono. From other sources it was ascertained that Rosenfeld was the monastery over which one Kuno presided until 1130.[1] There can be little doubt that Rosenfeld was the spot where the chronicle was compiled.

The immediate goal of external criticism, how-ever, is information about the personality of the author whose work has presumptive value as an historical source. He may be well known; his life history and methods of composition may be easily ascertained. In that case, the critical

[1] Bernheim, *Lehrbuch,* pp. 399–400.

scholar has only to pass rapidly to the evaluation of his writings. But what of the book, the pamphlet, the article, the manuscript which is anonymous? How may the authorship be determined?

At the outset it may be remarked that the discovery of the author's identity is less important than the revelation of his personal characteristics and social background: Whether the author was John Doe or Richard Roe makes little difference, provided the critic knows that John Doe was—let us say—an ignorant innkeeper with little direct knowledge of the events which he presumes to record, and that Richard Roe was an intelligent clerk, a witness of passing events, and a person of candid mind. The personal characteristics that make a writer a trustworthy witness or the reverse are of first importance. Hence the nationality of a writer should be ascertained—no very difficult matter ordinarily, but of some importance where political or diplomatic issues are involved. Vocation or official position often determines the nature of testimony. A burger of Mainz would be likely to have a different outlook from the bishop; a priest in the retinue of Count Raymond of Toulouse would narrate the events of the First

Crusade with a different emphasis from the anonymous crusader who wrote the *Gesta Francorum*. Party affiliations deflect testimony. It is essential to know whether an historian is Guelf or Ghibelline, Jacobin or Girondist, Democrat or Republican, Laborite or Liberal. And in all times and places religious predilections have colored accounts of the relations between church and state.

If a writing has been carefully dated and assigned to its place of origin, many important details about the personality of the author must have come to light. Peculiarities of handwriting, of language, and of composition can hardly fail to furnish clues to his nationality, and perhaps to his identity, while betraying personal allusions are almost certain to appear in the text, no matter how carefully an author may try to efface himself.

In the year 1879 *The North American Review* published extracts from the diary of "A Public Man" which give an intimate view of personalities at Washington in the transition from Buchanan's administration to Lincoln's. The identity of the diarist has never been disclosed; yet many convincing conjectures as to his personality and standing may be made. The writer was a man of public distinction. He had been long in residence at Washington. His contacts with the leading personages at the Capital were numerous. Though obviously a Northerner and a stanch Unionist, he was in touch with Southern leaders. He was recognized as a conservative and a lover of peace. He deplored the precipitancy of the Southern leaders. At the same time, he was a friend of Seward and on cordial and even confidential terms with Senator Douglas. He was treated with consideration by President Lincoln, whom he had met at Washington in 1848. He was greatly concerned about patent rights, trade relations, manufactures, and the tariff, in case a Southern Confederacy should be established. He had been a Whig; he was probably now a Republican and at this time a member of the Senate. "Washington, March 4. I never expected to experience such a sense of mortification and shame in my own country as I felt today in entering the Capitol through hedges of marines armed to the teeth. —— of Massachusetts, who felt as I did—indeed, I have yet to find a man who did not—recalled to me as we sat in the Senate-Chamber . . ." "March 7. Early this morning I received a message from the President, making an appointment for this afternoon. . . . In the Senate no one of the Republicans seems to be just now thinking seriously of anything but the new appointments. I have been besieged for a week past with letters and applications. . . ." With so much information about this diarist, the value of the record can be speedily determined. The identity of the writer becomes a matter of secondary interest.

The last inquiry in studying the external characteristics of an historical record is this: is it an original or a secondary source of information? Strictly speaking an original record would be one which contains the direct testimony of an eye-witness of events. All other accounts derived from this would be secondary sources. Usually, however, acccunts secured by contemporaries from eye-witnesses are treated as original sources. Contemporaneousness becomes the real test. If the authorship and date of a record have been settled conclusively, this last question will also have been answered, for inevitably the relation of writer to events recorded will be taken into consideration.

Not so simple, however, is the problem presented by the existence of two or more records which testify to the same events. The independence or relative dependence of these sources must be ascertained. Two or more original records will go far to establish the facts recorded; one will not, according to the canons which have yet to be examined. If A is an original source and B and C are derived from it, the weight of evidence is no greater than that contained in A. If A, B, and C are independent original sources, the historical probability of the events recorded is by so much stronger. In any case, the relation of A, B, and C must be determined.

If no light is thrown upon this relationship by these preliminary inquiries as to the date and authorship of A, B, and C, another test may be used, based upon self-evident axioms. Two persons, as every one knows, or may assure himself by simple tests, rarely see complicated happenings in exactly the same way. Never will they tell what they have seen in exactly the same language. Consequently if the details in a complicated series of events appear in the same order in two sources, one is probably derived from the other or both from a third. If in addition to this resemblance, there is an identity of literary form, the above conjecture becomes a certainty.

Assuming a connection between two sources, how can the exact relationship be determined? Which is the original? A conclusion will probably be reached by cumulative evidence. If the style is polished and elaborate in one source, and awkward and crude in the other; if the events are given a definite twist to convey an impression in one, and artlessly told in the other, the presumption is that the latter is the original source. The problem becomes more complicated where more than two sources are in question, and no hard and fast rules of procedure can be laid down.

No one can pursue the study of original sources far without discovering that not all are what they seem to be. Many a writer who seems to speak on his own authority as a contemporary is often only repeating what others have said. In the Middle Ages, and indeed well into our own times, the sense of literary property was not highly developed. Writers borrowed from one another without so much as a by-your-leave and rarely acknowledged their indebtedness, so that their productions are sometimes veritable mosaics, in which the spurious and the genuine are strangely mixed. Before such material can be used, of course, the component parts must be carefully separated, a task which often calls for a wide acquaintance with the literature of the period and a high degree of critical acumen.

Von Ranke won distinction by just such a study of Guicciardini's *Historia d'Italia,* one of the most famous histories of the sixteenth century.[1] Within fifty years after its publication, it had passed through ten editions in Italian, three in Latin, and three in French. It was translated into German, English, Dutch, and Spanish; and everywhere it was acclaimed as an authority of the first importance, because of the position of the author and his first-hand knowledge of events. Yet Von Ranke shows conclusively that even in those portions where Guicciardini was able to write as an observer of events, he borrowed from others and made their accounts his own. To take a single illustration: Guicciardini took over almost word for word the account of the Battle of Pavia as it was described by Galeazzo Capra in his history. Galeazzo's account appears to be far from accurate, yet Guicciardini makes no attempt to correct the errors, preferring the less painful method of transcribing the record bodily. Not only this: Von Ranke accuses Guicciardini of taking almost the whole of Galeazzo's fourth book and making it his fifteenth. And with equally slight regard to literary ethics as we understand the

[1] Leopold von Ranke, *Zur Kritik neuerer Geschichtsschreiber* (1824).

code, Guicciardini borrowed *ad libitum* from Bernardo Rucellai's *De bellis italicis* and Comines' memoirs. Bodin went out of his way to praise Guicciardini for the true speeches which he put into the mouths of the actors on his little stage, pointing out his superiority to those historians who merely invented them.[1] Von Ranke insists after patient study that of these speeches some were never delivered, others had undoubtedly been changed, and not one is genuine beyond reasonable doubt.

Not only plagiarisms beset the path of the historian but forgeries as well. The course of mediæval history is strewn with fabricated manuscripts and documents of all sorts. The motives for deception run through the whole gamut of human instincts and emotions, from love of gain to desire for revenge. Charters have been forged to secure grants of privileges or immunities; deeds, to secure claims to title or property; letters, to win personal or party advantage or to frustrate opponents; anecdotes and tales, to enhance or to damage reputations; stories, to excite wonder or to gratify a malicious desire to deceive; and documents of many kinds, to establish scholarly claims or to vindicate a theory.

[1] Bodin, *Methodus ad facilem historiarum cognitionem.*

The fabrication of antiques, as every one knows, has become one of the regular gainful occupations of craftsmen in the Mediterranean countries.[1]

An interesting example of mediæval forgery is the collection of papal letters and decretals attributed to Isidorus Mercator, which came into notice in the ninth century. Their authenticity was not called in question until the sixteenth. Under the successive assaults of critical scholars, ninety-four of the most important letters are now universally recognized as forgeries. The method of critical attack was, briefly stated, first to point out that the papal letters in question—supposedly written from the first to the eighth century—were all written in the same style. This style, further, was not that of some of the Popes, as a comparison with their well-authenticated letters proved. It was not difficult to show, too, that these letters drew upon some eighty different writings which dated only from the first part of the ninth century. It was also pointed out that many of these early papal letters were dated by the year of the Roman

[1] The reader will find much that is amusing as well as instructive in *The Gentle Art of Faking* (1921) by Riccardo Nobili; and in the older book by Robert Munro, *Archæology and False Antiquities* (1905).

consuls, a practice which was not in vogue until the end of the fourth century. Many similar stylistic anachronisms were proved. The contents also betrayed anachronisms. The western church as well as the eastern, for example, is represented in the first century as having its bishops, metropolitan sees, and provincial councils, when in point of fact such an organization was not attained in the west until much later. Through all these letters runs an evident desire to exalt the papal power.

One of the most arrant forgeries of mediæval manuscripts was the account of ancient Britain and the itinerary attributed to Richard of Cirencester. It was the fabrication of Charles Bertram, who successfully imposed upon the credulity of the then celebrated antiquarian, Doctor William Stukeley. Bertram sent to Stukeley copies of portions of a manuscript which he said that he had found, dating presumably from the fourteenth century. Subsequently he sent to Stukeley also a facsimile of some lines of the text and a map of ancient Britain. All of this material was pronounced genuine by English palæographers and antiquarians. In 1757 Bertram published, at Copenhagen, a small volume containing the text of Gildas and other chroniclers and his own forgery and map; and in the preface he had the audacity to declare that he was now publishing them "out of respect for Doctor Stukeley." It was not until the middle of the nineteenth century that suspicions of forgery were entertained; and meantime even historians like Lingard and Lappenberg had taken over many of the fictitious statements of Richard of Cirencester, while antiquarians quite generally had come to regard the map and itinerary as invaluable sources of information regarding the geography of ancient Britain. Finally, in a series of papers contributed to *The Gentleman's Magazine* in 1866 and 1867, B. B. Woodward, librarian of Windsor Castle, exposed the forgery beyond a doubt. The handwriting of Bertram's "facsimile" was shown to be inconsistent with itself and even to contain some modern letters; the Latin not only was not that of the fourteenth century, but often wholly fictitious, some words being a literal translation of English terms into supposititious Latin; and mistakes were made that could only have been committed by a person living as late as the eighteenth century. Yet so late as 1872 the unwary editor of *Six Old English Chronicles* included *The Ancient State of Britain*, by Richard of

Cirencester, "in the original Latin," with a detailed commentary upon the itinerary.[1] The original manuscript has never been found![2]

Forgeries of formal official documents are less common in modern times, partly because the modern mind is less credulous and partly because the means of detection are more complete. Yet forgeries of genealogies, memoirs, diaries, and letters are probably more numerous. A conspicuous instance, not without its amusing side, is *The Journal of a Spy in Paris During the Reign of Terror, January–July* 1794, by Raoul Hesdin. A critic in *The English Historical Review* pointed out numerous errors, and, though many of these could be explained in part at least by carelessness, boldly charged that the work was a forgery. Whereupon the author appeared in his own defense in several anonymous communications to *The Athenæum!* It is highly probable that *Memoirs of Cécile de Courtot*, by R. Kaisenberg, belong in the same class.

The *Eikon Basilike*, which purports to be the last message of King Charles I of England to his subjects, was almost certainly put together by

[1] *Six Old English Chronicles* (1872), in Bohn's Antiquarian Library.

[2] See article on Charles Bertram in the *Dictionary of National Biography.*

Doctor John Gauden, who indeed averred in the following reign that he was the author. A laborious critique in the London *Academy* points out that the writer of the *Eikon Basilike* was extremely fond of alliteration. Hundreds of instances occur. It is significant that in all Gauden's known works alliterative phrases and words abound. It was "almost a mania" with him, asserts the critic. Plays upon words occur frequently in the *Eikon* and in Gauden's writings. Then too, not one-sixth of the words used are found in King Charles's literary vocabulary, while phrases and expressions appear in the *Eikon* which are used by Gauden in other places, such as "Soul of our Souls," "the blessing of blessings temporal," and so on. Finally, it is alleged that the biblical quotations which are put into the king's mouth are precisely the favorite ones of Gauden.[1]

Interpolations in a text are always open to suspicion wherever they alter the original meaning. In the case of an original manuscript, a comparison of handwriting in the text and in the part under suspicion may lead to some positive conclusion. If the interpolated passage has been incorporated in the text of a copy, every effort

[1] I am indebted for the citation of C. E. Doble's articles in *The Academy*, to John M. Vincent's *Historical Research*, p. 109.

must be made to find the original, which may or may not contain the interpolation. Comparisons of style, form, and language must be made, as in the case of forgery, on a large scale. In short, the general rule is to compare the external form of the suspected passage with the rest of the text. Finally, the contents must be studied with the purpose of finding some motive for the interpolation, if indeed it is out of harmony with the rest of the text.

Such problems do not beset the path of the classical scholar or the mediævalist alone. Similar perplexities occur in the study of modern manuscripts. It is well known, for example, that next to the official *Journal*, the notes of the debates taken by James Madison are the most valuable source of information about the Federal Convention which framed the Constitution of the United States. These notes were first published in 1840; the *Journal* was published in 1819. It was commonly supposed that historians had thus two independent sources. It appears, however, that Madison used the printed *Journal* not only to correct some items in his notes, especially certain records of votes, but to insert matters relating to procedure which his own notes did not contain. To make matters worse,

Madison seems to have made two sets of corrections at two different times. It is a matter of more than antiquarian interest to know what these interpolations were, especially as the printed *Journal* is not infallible. The manuscript of Madison's notes is here all important. "The ink," writes the editor of the *Records of the Federal Convention*, "which was used at the later date has faded quite differently from that of the original notes, so that most of the later revisions stand out from the page almost as clearly as if they had been written in red ink." "This is not always the case, for the original manuscript has faded differently in different parts, perhaps because of different exposure or the use of more than one kind of ink. There also seem to have been at least two distinct sets of later corrections, probably made at different times. It is, therefore, sometimes difficult and sometimes impossible to determine whether or not the correction is a later one. A reference to the 'printed *Journal*' must of course be of a later date than 1819, and the ink and writing of these words will frequently make clear all of the corrections of that date. It is also very helpful to know that it was Madison's invariable practice in his original notes to refer to himself as 'M' or 'Mr.

M.' In the revision of his manuscript he filled out his own name, so that the ink and writing of 'adison' often furnish the necessary clue."[1]

From the historian's viewpoint there is no dividing line between a forgery and a hoax. The motive of the deception, except as it helps to explain the document, does not concern him. It is well to bear in mind, however, that deception may occur where malicious or gainful intent is not in the least to be suspected. A pamphlet which purports to have been printed at Boston in 1849 seems to have caused a little flurry among English scientists. It bears the title *Shall We Have Common Sense? Some Recent Lectures Written and Delivered by Geo. W. Sleeper*, and anticipates in a general way Darwin's theory of natural selection and the germ theory of disease. It was deemed of sufficient importance to be printed by the Linnæan Society of London.[2] Prolonged search, however, failed to discover another copy of the pamphlet; and though it purported to be registered in the District Court of Massachusetts, no entry was found in the records. This unique copy was said to have

[1] Max Farrand, *The Records of the Federal Convention of* 1787, vol. I, Introduction, p. xviii and note 23.

[2] *Proceedings* of the Linnæan Society of London, 1913–14.

been found in a bookshop in either Cincinnati or Cleveland, which cannot be found. No such type-face as that used on the title-page was in existence before 1870, according to the judgment of experts. In short, circumstantial evidence points to either a forgery or a hoax, but the author has escaped identification.

Through this laborious process of critical analysis runs one dominating purpose: to sweep away all disguises, all pretences, all falsifications, in order to stand face to face with the author of the manuscript or document in question.[1] Under the most favorable conditions he may be made to tell much about himself. If he will not disclose his personal identity, he may reveal his status and his relation to the news he tells. He will appear either as an eye-and-ear witness (as a contemporary) or as a mere teller of tales that he has heard from others; as a primary authority or as a secondary authority, in short. But whether the impression that his words convey is true or false, has still to be ascertained. The appraisal of his testimony has yet to be made.

[1] "Die Kritik strebt stets auf die erste Quelle zurückzugehen." Von Sybel in his *Gedächtnisrede auf Leopold v. Ranke* (1886). *Historische Zeitschrift*, 1886.

CHAPTER IV

THE ASSESSMENT OF EVIDENCE

There is a certain fascination in unravelling historical problems. No one with historical interests can remain insensible to the thrill that comes from unmasking an author who thought to hide his identity under a pseudonym. The dating of a significant document is a good deal like a game of wits with an unknown adversary. Yet these are, after all, only preliminary moves in a larger game. A seemingly important source of information has been found; it has been dated with reasonable accuracy; its author—at least, the personality of its author—is known. In short it is what it appears to be; it is authentic; it is genuine. What then? May the information contained in the document or record now be used with complete assurance? That depends upon circumstances, upon further internal examination. For a vital question remains to be answered: What is the source worth as historical evidence? [1]

[1] "Die innere Kritik hat die Tatsächlichkeit der Ereignisse zu bestimmen, indem sie beurteilt, wie sich die Quellenzeugnisse dazu verhalten. Ihre Aufgabe ist durchaus mit der eines Untersuchungsrichters zu ver-

It is a common assumption that the sources classified as remains are more trustworthy than records. The subjective factor, it is said, is likely to deflect all human testimony; but things cannot lie. What Livy wrote about the early history of Rome may be vitiated by a hundred doubts; but the remains in the Roman Forum speak for themselves. So stated, the argument seems cogent. The archæologist seems to stand on more solid ground than the mere historian who pores over documents. Yet a moment's reflection will expose a fallacy in this reasoning. "Things," remains, must be perceived and apprehended. If they have a meaning, it is because the archæologist or the historian discovers it. Remains are not vocal. At best they are mute witnesses. Their testimony must be wrested from them; it is not given. Remains, in short, must be interpreted by active intelligence.

It has already been remarked that "remains" is an all-inclusive term. Every form of historical record is—quite apart from its contents—an example of human activity. From this point of view manuscripts may be regarded as remains

gleichen, welcher die Tatsächlichkeit eines Vergehens aus Zeugenaussagen und aus unmittelbaren Spuren desselben zu konstatieren hat." Bernheim, *Lehrbuch*, p. 464.

quite as much as fragments of pottery. They may reveal the skilful artistry and manual dexterity of the scribe as well as the literary craftsmanship of the author, and to this extent may bear witness to the artistic level of the age. From this point of view again, all public and private documents—statutes, proclamations, despatches, protocols, tax-lists, accounts, wills, inventories, and what-not—are remains which attest the ways of chanceries and exchequers, or of commercial houses, legislative bodies, and courts of law.

How, then, the report of the Milanese envoy, Soncino, who sent home an account of King Henry VII and one Zoanne Caboto in the year 1497, shall be treated, depends wholly on the historian's interest and point of view. If he is trying to unravel the mystery that shrouds the voyages of the Cabots, he will scan the contents of this despatch with consuming eagerness; if, on the other hand, he is primarily interested in institutions he may find the despatch more interesting as an illustration of the fidelity of the envoys of these northern Italian city-states and of the ways of their diplomatic service. In the latter case, the document, once its authenticity is attested, is direct prima facie evidence of

Milanese diplomatic customs and usages. The only needful precaution would be to make sure that this despatch is fairly typical. There is, therefore, hardly a record of any description which may not have a value by reason of its mere survival, aside from the testimonial value of its contents.

Not quite so simple is the evaluation of memorials. They, by their very nature, stand half-way between remains and records. Both intentionally and unintentionally they transmit intelligence. The sarcophagus of Napoleon I in the Hôtel des Invalides is an interesting monument from many points of view. Considered merely as a mortuary monument, it may be taken to reflect the taste of the time. Ages hence it may testify, like the tombs of Egyptian Pharaohs, to the care of the dead in the nineteenth century. It may even record dates otherwise lost to history. But the sarcophagus of Napoleon bears not only testimony as to dates but an inscription: *Je désire que mes cendres reposent sur les bords de la Seine, au milieu de ce peuple français que j'ai tant aimé.* Here obviously enters the subjective element. The memorial has a purpose; it would perpetuate an interpretation of the career of the Emperor. As such, the inscription is an interesting bit of testimony to the growth of a Napoleonic cult.

The study of historical inscriptions thus bridges the gap between remains and records. So far as they state bald facts of an official sort, such as the names and dates of rulers, of battles, of disasters, which were matters of common knowledge, they have almost as little of the subjective element as the material upon which they are carved.[1] But the instant inscriptions pass beyond the bare enumeration of such universally known facts and add comments on events, they become records which must be tested just as rigorously as chronicles.

Genealogical lists, ancient or modern, are particularly open to doubt. There is hardly a human motive which may not be found in compilations of such records, from family pride to love of lucre. The traffic in genealogies, particularly in America, where every parvenu desires a family tree, has assumed extraordinary proportions.

[1] Even here, it should be remarked, there is a natural tendency to record only the events which reflect glory upon the reigning monarch or upon the nation. Writing of inscriptions on Egyptian graves and temples, Eduard Meyer remarks: "Naturally, only glorious deeds are recorded, unfortunate matters passed over in silence, and generally speaking only things interesting to the inscriber are brought forward." *Geschichte des Altertums*, I, p. 31.

No hard and fast line can be drawn, then, between records which may be taken at their face value and records which must be winnowed and sifted before the kernels of truth can be found. The instant that the desire to transmit intelligence appears in source material, the historian must be on his guard. Historical information transmitted by an active intelligence is bound to be somewhat deflected from the exact truth. No human mind is infallible. Every man is a child of the age, a creature of his environment, and subject to conditions of time and place. What these conditions are in any given case must always be ascertained. There remains the further question whether the narrator of historical happenings desired to tell the truth.

There are reporters of facts, eye-witnesses of events, who inspire no confidence, not because they lack training and intelligence or habits of accurate observation, but because they do not care for truth. Unless an observer wills to tell the truth so far as he can see it, he may as well be ignored as a trustworthy authority. It becomes a matter of primary importance, then, to determine the moral character of an historical witness. How can this be done?

Obviously, asseverations of honesty do not always carry conviction. More than the avowed purpose of telling the truth is needed. The tone and spirit of an historical writing must be taken into account. And if other writings than the one under consideration can be found, these too should be given a careful scrutiny. An author who betrays his willingness to sacrifice the truth in one instance can hardly be trusted in another.

It was in this wise that the late Professor Catterall laid bare the untrustworthiness of Marat. Biographies had hitherto been based upon material furnished by Marat himself. Much of this material was accepted at its face value because there was no way of testing its accuracy. But if other writings by Marat could be tested, these might reveal his truthfulness or the lack of it. A careful study of a pamphlet called *The Chains of Slavery*, published at London in 1774, convinced Professor Catterall that it was written by Marat, as indeed he frankly avowed twenty years later, when a French version was published at Paris. To this Paris edition he prefixed an account of the circumstances under which he wrote the English version. This account abounds in untruths. Marat asserts, for example, that the newspapers refused to print notices of the publication of the book, although he offered as much as ten guineas for such notices. But several notices have been found in London papers. Equally false is his story that Lord North suppressed the book lest it should cost him his majority in the next House of Commons. "Marat," concludes Professor Catterall, "is guilty then of telling us a story about the publication of his book in England which is false in almost every particular where we can control his assertions, and finally he shows himself unable to tell the exact truth in a matter where there was no motive for falsehood and no difficulty in stating the facts as they were. Consequently, it is impossible to credit his statements in cases where there is no corroborative evidence for them." [1]

The process of evaluating records can be best illustrated in the case of memoirs, which, as every one knows, are the most unreliable of all historical records. The writer of memoirs seldom has a purely scientific purpose in view. He rarely writes as a dispassionate observer of events or as a detached critic of his contemporaries. Whatever his motive, he writes out of the fulness of his own experience—or at least he would have

[1] R. C. H. Catterall, "The Credibility of Marat," in *The American Historical Review,* October, 1910.

his readers so believe. If he does not exclaim with Æneas, "quorum pars magna fui," it is because he leaves this easy inference to his readers. He may not himself have been a conspicuous actor in the stirring drama of his times; he may have been content to pull the strings of puppets on his stage, or even merely to be the *fidus Achates* of some hero. In any case he has had—so he would have his readers believe—unusual opportunities to know that whereof he writes.

The historian must run through the whole gamut of motives to find the dominant purpose of the writer of memoirs. Thirst for literary distinction is quite as often the impelling motive as thirst for gold, though they are not mutually exclusive. In the memoirs of statesmen and politicians, the desire to justify conduct or a course of action is often uppermost. To set posterity right on misunderstood events is the anxious wish of many who have suffered contumely in the grim battle of life. But first, last, and always, the writer would make clear the part he has taken in the events of his time.

The intermingling of motives in the writing of Walpole's *Memoirs of George the Third* has been clearly delineated by Professor Carl Becker. "It cannot be supposed that he [Horace Walpole] was ever indifferent to fame. . . . What he despised was the professional hack writer, hat in hand before some noble patron or other. . . . To be known as a lazy trifler whose cleverness enabled him to throw off many books without effort, was well enough; even if he did no more than fashion odd curios of literature, interesting to 'men of parts,' no one could say that he had failed, since he had never had high aims. It was not indifference to fame, but the sensitive fear of having loved and lost, that is at the root of Walpole's literary pose. Writing was the business of his life, and he wrote the memoirs partly because he found the business of his life amusing, and had, always, to be writing something. . . . Nevertheless, Walpole had undoubtedly a more serious purpose than amusement: he wrote for posterity. . . . In the next century, at least, they would know that he, Walpole, already old and half-forgotten by the young of his own generation, knew better than any one what was going on, and had a finger in the pie, although he pulled out no plums." [1]

First of all, then, the motive or motives of a writer of memoirs must be laid bare before they

[1] "Horace Walpole's Memoirs of the Reign of George the Third," by Carl Becker, in *The American Historical Review*, vol. 16, pp. 501–2.

can be used as sources. The point does not need elaboration, for, if the work of external criticism has been well done, the facts of the author's personality are now patent and his point of view well understood. Hardly less important is it to know the circumstances under which the memoirs were written. Was the author writing after a considerable lapse of time or immediately after the occurrences which he describes? In the latter case, though the narrative may lack perspective, it may have greater fulness and vividness of detail; in the former case, it may be subtly distorted by vicissitudes in the writer's own life. Any turn in the wheel of life may give the writer a new retrospect of remote events. Prosperity may have given him an optimistic and charitable outlook upon historical happenings which otherwise might have a sinister aspect. Bodily infirmities, mental depression, business reverses, are likely to dull the edge of memory. In evaluating memoirs, then, the personal experiences of the writer should be carefully noted and, of course, the ongoing of public affairs never lost from view.

A better illustration of the problem could hardly be found than in these same memoirs of Horace Walpole. They were written supposedly between 1766 and 1772; but "transcribed" by the author in 1775, and enlarged by the addition of new matter in 1784. The point of view of the author in 1784—after the American Revolution—is in marked contrast to opinions expressed in his letters before 1775. The interesting query then rises: How far did Walpole alter his earlier views in this revision? The whole series of problems thus suggested is handled with great subtlety by Professor Becker. His conclusions are summarized as follows:

In the original draft Walpole was intent on details, and wished to picture the particular person or situation, and himself most of all; in the revision of 1784, he was intent on principles and general tendencies, and wished to picture the whole reign as a lesson to posterity. In the interval between the writing of the original draft and the revision of 1784, Walpole had changed in more respects than in his view of the meaning of the reign of George III; his attitude toward the function of the historian, and toward his own memoirs and the purposes they might serve, had changed also. Whether Walpole's later view of the reign of George III is a truer one on the whole than his earlier view, is a question that might be argued but cannot be argued here. At least, that he had an earlier and a later view is obvious, and it is perhaps well to know that he did." [1]

A searching inquiry of this sort is bound to answer another scarcely less important question: whether the author wrote from memory or based his narrative on notes and letters contemporary with the events. Enough has been said of the instability of unaided memory. Yet the accuracy of memoirs based upon a journal or diary is not to be taken for granted. The investigation must simply be carried one step farther. How, when, and under what circumstances was the diary or journal written? Unfortunately, it does not follow that diaries with their day by day entries are chronologically infallible. The most methodical diarist nods and permits gaps to occur, and is often sorely tempted to write in, under a given date, not what he then knew, but what he subsequently learned. An interesting example of this sort of interpolation may be found in the journal of Prince Karl of Rumania, the younger brother of that Prince Leopold of Hohenzollern whose candidacy for the throne of Spain was the immediate occasion for the Franco-Prussian War of 1870–71. Through family letters Prince Karl was kept in close touch with the negotiations,

[1] *Ibid.*, p. 507.

and his journal becomes thus a source of first-rate importance. Every move in these negotiations must be correlated with the current happenings in the surcharged diplomatic atmosphere of 1870, if the provocative character of the Hohenzollern candidacy is to be understood. Prince Karl writes under date of June 4th: "The hereditary Prince of Hohenzollern has declared himself ready to accept the Spanish crown, since he has been assured by those best informed that the interest of the state demands this course. He has determined to dismiss all personal considerations and to yield to higher necessity; in this sense he has written to the King of Prussia. . . . King William has had a conference with the Czar of Russia at Ems."

But further evidence points clearly to the fact that Leopold did not announce his acceptance until the offer had been repeated (sometime after June 14th). Now, since King William was in Ems on the 21st of June for the second time, it seems probable that Prince Karl wrote in under date of June 4th, when King William was first at Ems, what happened on the King's second visit. Obviously the student who uses this journal cannot place implicit confidence in its chronology.

Very few diaries, moreover, have been kept without some thought of posterity. There may be rare souls who find joy merely in private self-expression or who make their diaries their confessional, with never a side-glance at the reader waiting far down on the edge of time; but the presumption is always against such lofty isolation. The diary of a man who is, or who has been, in public life is almost inevitably *une pièce justificative.* Rarely can he refrain from justifying his conduct or from magnifying his own part in public events. The diary of John Quincy Adams was kept with meticulous care, so that his children might know the mighty deeds of their sire. Yet historians have persisted in using these twelve volumes of *Memoirs* as though they contained the last word on the events in which Adams had a part. That Adams often wrote late at night, when overcome with bodily and mental fatigue and when consequently he was no fair judge of either men or events, seems to have escaped many historians. Under these cirstances, Adams's portraits of his contemporaries are frequently no better than caricatures; and his accounts of daily happenings are strongly colored by his own prejudices and by his ever-present regard for the opinions of posterity.

No matter how perseveringly an historian may press back to original sources, he cannot afford to ignore the work of historians who may have preceded him. Formal histories and biographies may themselves be original sources, either by reason of material which has been incorporated in them and which can be found nowhere else, or by reason of a point of view which is itself historically valuable. The point hardly needs emphasis so far as ancient and mediæval histories are concerned. Our knowledge of Greek history in the fifth century before Christ would be slight indeed without Herodotus and Thucydides; the early contact of Rome with the Teutonic peoples of Western Europe would have been more conjectural than it is without Cæsar and Tacitus; the history of Charlemagne could hardly be reconstructed without the annalists and Einhard.

At the risk of tiresome reiteration, it may again be said that the historical student should be on his guard against the motivation of biographies and histories. No rapid skimming of a preface will suffice, for the author is often sublimely unconscious of the tendency or bias which may vitiate his historical work. On the other hand, this bias may itself be an historical fact of some importance. A biography written while the memory of a great personage is still green may bear strong testimony to the charm of his personality, even though it exaggerates his part in the history of his times and distorts a whole sequence of events.

The impersonal character of public and private documents would seem to set them apart from the historical sources just considered. Assured of their literal accuracy, the historian surely need have no further concern. A statute is a statute; an ordinance is an ordinance; a proclamation is a proclamation; a deed is a deed; and a will is a will. What possible subjective element can creep into such documents which would weaken their value as historical evidence? There are, indeed, fewer pitfalls for the unwary in writing the history of institutions—the collective ways of social groups; yet even official documents may be misleading, sometimes designedly misleading. The preamble of a statute, for example, may set forth reasons for its enactment which are wholly untrue. The title of an act may conceal its real significance and so become a defense of the lawmakers. The first reconstruction act passed by the American Congress, in 1867, bore the title, "An Act to Provide for the More Efficient

Government of the Rebel States"; and it began with the words, "Whereas no legal State governments or adequate protection for life or property now exists in the rebel States of . . .; and whereas it is necessary that peace and good order should be enforced in said States until loyal and republican State governments can be legally established. . . ." As President Andrew Johnson pointed out in a vigorous veto message, not the establishment of peace and order, but the establishment of negro suffrage was the real object of the bill. Seven of these ten States, moreover, had been regarded as legal to the extent that their votes had been accepted in counting the necessary three-fourths majority for the adoption of the thirteenth amendment to the Constitution.

Apropos of the statute of 1536 abolishing monasteries, Professor Vincent remarks trenchantly that no historian of the present generation would, like Mr. Froude, believe the allegations in the preamble simply because they were there stated. Most historians are now convinced that the lawmakers were impressed by other, less worthy, motives than a desire to do away with "sin, vicious, carnal, and abominable living" in the abbeys and priories of England.

The preamble is interesting, however, as a justification, and has its place as historical material; but it is of a different sort from the body of the act.[1]

An act on the statute book, moreover, is not in itself alone sufficient evidence of the offences which it forbids. The whims of legislators have in our day become a subject of jest. And it hardly need be said that the existence of laws bears no relation whatever to the conformity of the public to their precepts. The repeated enactment of statutes regulating labor in the age of Elizabeth and of sumptuary laws elsewhere is not evidence of public obedience but rather of the contrary.

Proclamations and public announcements are not always to be taken at their face value. They may be partisan pronunciamentos, part of a skilful official propaganda, and in time of war a means of deceiving the enemy. Diplomatic documents are, above all, open to suspicion. The public text of a treaty may have a different meaning when read in connection with secret articles which have been omitted for prudential reasons.

The modern world possesses in the newspaper

[1] John M. Vincent, *Historical Research,* pp. 171–2.

a source of historical information which is unique. Although news-letters and even news-sheets circulated in the seventeenth century, the newspaper in anything like its present form dates no farther back than the early eighteenth century. It was a product of the printing press; and its modern development is due mainly to improvements in the technique of printing and in the means of communication. The contrast between the diminutive four-page newspaper of the eighteenth century and the massive metropolitan newspaper of the twentieth suggests both the rapid evolution of society since the industrial revolution and the multiplication of news interests. The earlier news-sheets, laboriously printed by hand once a week, contained largely news from a distance—foreign news; the modern daily appeals to manifold interests, touches life intimately on all its sides, and prospers commercially because it serves the public in innumerable ways.

The news columns of a typical metropolitan daily in England or America touch on a wide variety of subjects: domestic and foreign politics; commerce, manufacturing, mining, farming, building, shipping, transportation; banking, stock markets, investments; crime; sports; the theatre; the army and navy; churches, schools, colleges, fraternal organizations, trade unions; weather reports; social and personal news; scientific discoveries and inventions. And to this mass of information, editors add their leaders and book reviewers their estimates of current literature, while syndicated articles on every conceivable subject appear as fillers. Finally, chief source of revenue for the modern newspaper, paid notices and advertisements add enormously to the bulk of these ephemeral publications.

The mere enumeration of the contents of a typical daily demonstrates the futility of passing judgment on *the* newspaper as a source of historical information. To discuss "the authenticity of the newspaper" or "the personality of the newspaper" leads nowhere, for what a paper prints as news is no more trustworthy than the source from which it comes.[1] A daily issue is the product of many minds and pens. And a wholesome scepticism must possess the mind of every one who would use newspapers as an historical source. Dismissing the possibility of giving a

[1] In spite of the mass of interesting information in Miss Lucy Salmon's two volumes on the newspaper, the real problem of the historian is not duly emphasized. See *The Newspaper and Authority* and *The Newspaper and the Historian* (1923).

blanket indorsement to any newspaper, the historian must weigh every news item for what it is worth.

Many important features of the newspaper are supplied from official sources and are therefore free from any suspicion of fraud though not of occasional error. Weather reports, shipping news, calendars of courts, proclamations, election notices, notices of recorded transfers of property, building permits, notices of bids for contracts, are typical examples of matter which may be accepted at its face value. Almost equally authoritative and trustworthy are stock market reports, banking statistics, and foreign exchange statements. Accuracy in such items is so vital to the sponsors that the liability of error is very slight.

In almost all other respects the newspaper is what it in early days so often called itself—an intelligencer. Its contents must be subjected to all the tests which critical scholarship applies to the kinds of historical sources already noted. Accounts of the earthquake in Japan and of riots in the Ruhr Valley—so-called contemporary events—must be treated precisely as the historian treats the Roman descriptions of the destruction of Pompeii, and the Reign of Terror in France. It has been said that news-collecting agencies, which have had an astounding development since the middle of the last century, have given authoritativeness to news. That they have exercised a wholesome control over irresponsible reporters is undoubtedly true. That they have taken precautions to sift truth from fiction may not be doubted. Yet such organizations must depend in last analysis on the individual reporter and no corporative control can make him infallible. An Associated Press despatch from the scene of a disaster is not necessarily more trustworthy than an account by a reporter on the staff of an independent newspaper.

The interview, one of the unique contributions of modern journalism, has not been regarded as a valuable source of information for historical purposes. The interviewer is too often obviously exploiting his victim in order to make good copy for his paper. The reading public, he knows, would rather be amused and diverted than instructed. The information which he has not been able to extract, he may supply with ready wit. And instances of faked interviews have become so frequent as to arouse a general scepticism in a usually credulous public. The collective interview, however, in which many reporters waylay the same individual, may yield some valuable data to the historian. Each is to some extent a check upon the exuberance of the others.

In view of what has been said of the necessity of thorough-going scepticism in examining testimony, it is hardly necessary to insist upon the need of corroborative evidence in newspaper reports. Yet even the best of historians yield to that subtle pressure which is exerted by the printed page. So easy is it to imagine that the newspaper speaks with unimpeachable authority because it seems to be so much bigger than any human personality. An excellent illustration of the danger of hasty judgment based on a single newspaper report is found in Mr. James Ford Rhodes's description of Calhoun on the occasion of his speech on the compromise resolutions—March 4, 1850.[1] "Long battle with disease had wasted his frame," writes Mr. Rhodes, "but, swathed in flannels, he crawled to the Senate Chamber. . . . He was too weak to deliver his carefully written speech. At his request, it was read by Senator Mason." On this latter point all authorities agree. "Calhoun," continues Mr. Rhodes, citing Charles A. Dana's report to the

[1] Rhodes, *History of the United States,* I, p. 127.

New York *Tribune*, "sat, with head erect and eyes partly closed, immovable in front of the reader; and he did not betray a sense of the deep interest with which his friends and followers listened to the well-matured words of their leader and political guide." But the reporter of the Charleston *Mercury* saw a different picture.[1] "His [Calhoun's] step, as he came in, seemed almost as firm and elastic as ever, but he looks quite emaciated." Calhoun remained seated during the reading, continues this eye-witness, "his eyes moving about his audience to note its effect.[2] The most interesting spectacle was presented after the Senate adjourned. There was [*sic*] Clay, Calhoun, and Webster standing together for some time near the speaker's desk, and conversing about his speech." Just how a person who had just been able to crawl into the Senate Chamber could stand and converse in this fashion does not appear. The discrepancy in these reports is obvious. And it need not be assumed that if Dana's despatch had been published by an Associated Press it would have gained in authenticity.

[1] Charleston *Mercury*, March 9, 1850.

[2] "Calhoun sat immovable . . . not a change passed over the muscles of his face," reported Dana, New York *Tribune*, March 6, 1850.

The quintessence of the whole process of historical criticism is contained in Von Sybel's memorial address on Von Ranke, and particularly in the following words: "Every narrator of events reports to us not the events themselves, but the impression which he has received of them. In this process of representation, however, there is always mingled, after an experience, a subjective element; and to retain the true picture of events by eliminating this subjective element is the task of historical criticism." [1]

[1] Von Sybel, *Gedächtnisrede auf Leopold v. Ranke,* in *Historische Zeitschrift,* 1886.

CHAPTER V

THE EVOLUTION OF METHOD

An art or a science does not formulate the rules of its technique until it becomes independent and self-conscious. So long as history was regarded as a branch of philosophy or rhetoric or oratory, no one felt the need of observing any special rules of technique apart from grammar or formal logic. Only when circumstances gave history an acknowledged rôle apart from other sciences or arts, were any attempts made to formulate rules of historical method; and these circumstances did not occur until the seventeenth century.[1] They were of many kinds. The study of classical antiquity had revived interest in the forgotten Greek and Roman histories. Men began to acquire a certain historical sense—a feeling of continuity between the ancient world and their own. The religious revolt of the sixteenth century led to a zealous searching of

[1] Several writers in the early seventeenth century anticipate this differentiation of history from other subjects, but G. J. Voss is the first, in his *Ars historica* (1623), to state effectively the claims of history as an independent subject of study. These early works contribute little or nothing to methodology, so far as problems of evidence are concerned.

ecclesiastical records, of the writings of the church fathers, and of the lives of the saints, rather, it must be admitted, to find arguments to vanquish opponents than to establish the truths of history. Yet the outcome was a measurable increase of interest in historical study.

Controversies within the church, particularly among the religious orders, also sent Benedictines, Bollandists, and Jesuits to historical sources, in order to vindicate privileges or to establish matters of doctrine and discipline. It was the attacks of the Lutheran reformer, Matthias Flacius, in his *Historia ecclesiæ Christi*, which aroused Cæsar Baronius to begin his monumental *Annales ecclesiastici*. It was the animadversions of the Jesuits that prompted the Benedictines of Saint-Maur to undertake the publication of the *Acta sanctorum* of their order. And it was the attacks of a Bollandist on the authenticity of their early charters which made Jean Mabillon, editor of the *Acta sanctorum*, their protagonist. The brethren of Saint-Maur had besought him to reply in militant fashion; but Brother Jean chose the better way.[1] He set to

[1] S. Bäumer, *Johannes Mabillon* (1892), pp. 79 ff. See also E. de Broglie, *Mabillon et la société de l'abbaye de S. Germain des Prés*, 1664–1707 (1888), 2 v.

work upon a manual which should lay down once for all the criteria by which spurious charters could be distinguished from genuine. The outcome was a folio bearing the title *De re diplomatica*, printed in 1681, the first treatise on methodology, and still a classic work on diplomatics. It contains not only a careful exposition of the way in which charters were prepared, but a minute description of the material and the ink used, and of the handwriting characteristic of different chanceries. Sixty specimens of handwriting and over two hundred documents were added as *pièces justificatives*. "In the place of arbitrary suppositions and conjectures, Mabillon put well-founded rules, based on material of singularly rich content." [1]

Two years later the brothers of Saint-Maur again appealed to Mabillon to repel an assault from another quarter. The aggressor this time was a Trappist reformer, who in an excess of zeal deprecated all monastic studies. Monks should fill their hours with prayer, worship, and labor, not with study of books and manuscripts. Mabillon's reply was a book printed in 1691 with the title *Traité des études monastiques*. It has a place in the history of methodology because of

[1] W. Wattenbach, *Das Schriftwesen im Mittelalter* (1871), pp. 13, 15.

its eighth chapter, where Mabillon sets down considerations which should guide the reader of history. One should read trustworthy historians so far as possible; that is, historians who are honest, unbiassed, and accurate. But since one must often use prejudiced historians, for want of better, a reader should learn how to distinguish the true and the false in their writings. But how may one know what historians are trustworthy? Make sure first, Mabillon advises, that a historian is not a mere copyist, but an original, contemporary authority—though, to be sure, a copyist is not to be despised if he has corrected or explained an original authority, or if the original authority has been lost. Then, one should look for a certain honesty (*probité*) in an historian, a quality which makes him incapable of wishing to impose on his readers by assuring them that he has seen or heard when he has neither seen nor heard what he records. Again, one should give preference to historians who have critical ability. It is not enough that a historian should not be a liar: he must possess judgment and accuracy, so as not on the one hand to believe and on the other not to disbelieve too readily. Finally, one should trust historians whom the church has approved and reject others. But as to those who have been put on the *Index*, adds Brother Jean with the cunning of the serpent, one should remember that they have been censured for certain errors. It is not necessary to believe that they are untrustworthy in other particulars!

More than a hundred years before Mabillon, Jean Bodin had written his *Methodus ad facilem historiarum cognitionem*, which has been described as an outstanding contribution to historical methodology. Why it should receive this encomium, I do not understand. Bodin was interested in history only for its bearing upon the science of jurisprudence; and aside from his discussion of sources and aids to history, he contributes little to the development of method. In spirit, to be sure, he is akin to the Cartesians of the next century, and there is a fine ring to the words *Non tam auctoritate, quae nihil valet apud eos qui ratione duci volunt, quam necessariis argumentis doceamus;*[1] but his observations on method are neither penetrating nor convincing. He observes, for example, that the testimony of a single witness must be tested by reason, a vague statement which leads nowhere, unless all sorts of meanings are read into this word reason. If

[1] *Methodus*, VIII, 362.

testimony be given by several persons, the true facts are best ascertained by comparison, with due regard to the personal qualities of the witnesses and to the manner in which they have conducted their inquiries; and that account (or fact) may be accepted as true upon which the witnesses agree, even though they disagree on all else. But Bodin seems to limit the application of this rule, and indeed to strip the foregoing observation of all its force, when he states elsewhere that even the agreement of several witnesses does not establish the truth, because men may err. It is difficult to make Bodin's comments self-consistent, unless one interpolates qualifying words and phrases to give precision to his thought—an exceedingly questionable undertaking.

Aside from the circumstances already noted, another force was insensibly shaping the trend of historical method in the seventeenth century. In 1637 René Descartes published his *Discours de la Méthode*, in which he affirmed the supremacy of reason and the immutability of the laws of nature. Carried to their logical conclusion, these principles had destructive consequences. What would become of the authority of the church? What of tradition, upon which so many dogmas of the church rested? What of the belief in an active Providence that was continually intervening in human history? Small wonder that the Cartesian philosophy found its chief opponents in the ranks of the theologians.

On the other hand, Cartesianism strengthened the hands of those who were already beginning to subject the history of the church and the lives of the saints to critical examination. Mabillon warned his readers against spurious lives of the saints; and he remarked with some asperity that the lives of pagans had often been written with more accuracy than the lives of saints. It was to the interest of the church, he urged, that the spurious should be separated from the genuine in the traditional hagiography. But this trend toward scepticism was combated vigorously, and perhaps held in check, by the Jansenists in France, and less resolutely by the Jesuits, for fifty years and more. The theory of an active Providence in human affairs was re-asserted with new vigor by Bossuet in his *Discours sur l'Histoire universelle*, published in 1681.

In the following century Cartesian ideas exerted an appreciable influence upon historical writing and gave rise, indirectly at least, to several notable treatises on historical method. Midway in this transition to modern thought is a book by Honoré de Sainte Marie, a Carmelite, printed in 1713, with the title *Reflexions sur les règles et sur l'usage de la critique.*[1] It was written to show how defective historical criticism is, why it is so defective, and what might be done to correct its faults. The author's main thesis is that historical truth cannot be reached by *la critique*, which he defines as the art of judging facts, because the means employed are inadequate. Mere authority and conjecture (by which the author means, I infer, testimony and inference) can only lead to error, unless they are supplemented by tradition and usage in the church; and the body of the book is made up of a series of dissertations which consider with wearisome prolixity the faults of critics in the field of ecclesiastical history. Permeated though the book is with a mediæval spirit, it sets forth certain rules of procedure which mark an advance in historical thinking. They may be stated summarily as follows:

As to well-known and not incredible events,

[1] The full title reads: *Reflexions sur les règles et sur l'usage de la critique, touchant l'histoire de l'église; les ouvrages des Pères; les Actes des anciens Martyrs; les Vies des Saints; & sur la Méthode qu'un écrivain a donnée pour faire une Version de la Bible plus exacte que tout ce qui a paru jusqu' à present.*

one should accept without question (*sans balancer*) the testimony of those writers under whose eyes they have happened, or who have learned of them from honest, trustworthy contemporaries living in the country where the events occurred. A "contemporary" is a person living in the same age.

As to events which are not public but which contain nothing fabulous, one should regard them as probable when they occur in the country of the writer, and highly probable when recounted by eye-witnesses or by contemporaries who do not seem to wish to deceive.

As to events which are "a little extraordinary," which occur in a foreign country, and which are known to few persons, one should not reject them without convincing proof, for it is unbelievable that an honest man would be impudent enough to report facts which any contemporary could prove false. This rule contains, of course, the familiar argument from silence, which vitiates a great deal of historical writing in the seventeenth century.

As to events of a public nature which are improbable and little known and which occur in a foreign country, one should not accept them "without examination"—a qualification which may mean much or little.

The author exhibits a similar mixture of sagacity and credulity in formulating rules of evidence. The testimony of a single witness, he insists, must be rejected in favor of that of several opposing witnesses if they are equally trustworthy; but when one or more writers recount a fact not mentioned by others, the former are to be followed, because writers often omit to mention things which happen under their very eyes. That this latter rule is not to be taken at quite its face value is clear from the following shrewd observation. When several writers report the same event in different ways, it is necessary to find out their several interests, "car l'intérêt séduit ordinairement les hommes."

An odd compound is this treatise by Honoré de Sainte Marie, a sort of Janus-faced production belonging to both past and future. And much the same thing may be said of a treatise by another theologian, Lenglet du Fresnoy, which was published in the same year. Like Mabillon's *Traité des études monastiques*, its title suggests that it was written for readers rather than writers of history: *Méthode pour étudier l'histoire.*[1] But

[1] The complete title runs: *Méthode pour étudier l'histoire où après avoir établi les principes & l'ordre qu'on doit tenir pour la lire utilement, on fait les remarques nécessaires pour ne se pas laisser tromper dans sa lecture.* Paris, 1713.

in fact it has many considerations to urge upon the serious student, the reader of original sources.

Du Fresnoy classifies aids to the study of history in a way that inspires confidence in his acumen. He is well aware of the dangers that lurk in the uncritical use of memoirs, letters, diplomatic documents, panegyrics, funeral sermons, and satires; and he declares that charters are "infinitely more necessary" to the historian, though these may well be supplemented by the use of inscriptions, medals, and coins. He is outspoken in his earnest warning against spurious patristic writings and sets down categorically rules for detecting forgeries. They may be paraphrased briefly in this wise: Consider as forged or doubtful (1) those writings attributed to the Apostles or to the Fathers of the first century which were unknown in that age or immediately after; (2) those writings which the Fathers so considered in the first century; (3) those writings that mention persons who lived later, or ceremonies, manners, and customs which arose later, or that discuss heresies and doctrines of a later date; (4) writings which contain errors that the alleged author would not have committed, or fables and falsehoods which he would not have told; (5) every writing which has a style alien to the time of its pretended origin as shown by comparison with writings of undoubted authenticity.

Confidence in Du Fresnoy as a methodologist wanes, however, when we turn to his rules for evaluating evidence. Then the theologian is more in evidence than the critic. To say that the possibility of an event is not in itself sufficient ground for holding that it occurred, is to stress the obvious; and Du Fresnoy does not give any greater point to the statement by adding that one must consider "external circumstances," for he does not explain what the phrase means. An event or fact sufficiently attested, he continues, must be considered possible or probable, in the absence of evidence to the contrary; but an event or fact is sufficiently attested in his judgment, as he goes on to prove to his satisfaction, when it is a tradition of the church. No one can prove that St. Peter did not visit Rome by saying that none of the church fathers nor St. Paul mentions his presence in the city, for this is one of the most positive facts of history and those who deny it must show that it is contrary to the Scriptures. Quite in line with this reasoning is a third rule: piety does not require a man of good sense to believe all miracles reported; but it does require him to believe those reported by St. Augustine, for it cannot be believed that that holy man would resort to falsehood to spread the faith, especially when there were innumerable witnesses to reveal his untruthfulness.

One is tempted, after this lapse into mere dogmatism, to dismiss Du Fresnoy without further consideration, when attention is arrested by this illuminating comment: even doubtful or false facts, he remarks, may have a certain value, if the motives of the writers and the circumstances under which they wrote are understood. It may happen that instead of circumstances producing a belief, belief produced the circumstances. Even supposititious miracles, when reported by the Fathers and commonly believed, prove the general prevalence of faith at the time. And still another statement goes far to restore Du Fresnoy's credit. Even prejudiced writers should not be cast aside as worthless, he pleads: one should ascertain their prejudices and then discriminate between facts which arouse and facts which do not arouse these prejudices. For, if we exclude rigorously all historians who exhibit bias, we must abandon the study of history, "parcequ'il n'y a point d'homme assez dégagé de lui-même, pour ne pas se laisser emporter quelquefois par la passion ou par quelque intérêt" (p. 463).

A more precise formulation of the rules of historical evidence did not appear for half a century. It was a Jesuit, Henri Griffet, himself a historian, who in 1769 published *Traité des différentes sortes de preuves qui servent à établir la vérité de l'histoire*, the most significant book on method after Mabillon's *De re diplomatica.* Father Griffet divides writers of history into four classes: contemporary historians; modern historians; abbreviators of history; compilers of history. The first of these have the best opportunity to know the truth: it is under their very eyes. But contemporaries often fail to see the truth because of their prejudices or their negligence. Moreover, they are often misled by rumor, and report not what they have seen but what they have been told. Modern historians must depend largely on the testimony of contemporary writers, hence the nature of the problem with which every such historian must grapple. The modern historian—Griffet is the first writer to use the analogy—is like a judge in court who must confront witnesses, examine them, and ascertain the truth by painstaking study and comparison of the evidence. He must ever carry in his hand the torch of criticism in order to determine the trustworthiness of witnesses—to reject them when false, to reconcile them when contradictory (p. 3).

Another means of getting at the truth is by the use of original and authentic records (*pièces*), by which Griffet means state papers or official records. The authority of such material he regards as superior to all other historical sources (pp. 192, 213–4). The testimony of a contemporary writer cannot hold against the precise text of authentic records. The agreement of contemporary testimony and authentic records, on the other hand, constitutes complete historical proof and establishes the truth of the facts in question (p. 215).

Taken all in all this is the most clear-cut statement of the fundamentals of historical research that can be found in the French literature of the eighteenth century. Upon this foundation Griffet erects his superstructure of method. First of all, before a historian may use a contemporary writer, he should make sure that this contemporary is really the author of the book which bears his name, for it is a common practice to borrow famous names and many fraudulent writings are current. Next, one should make sure that the writer was in a position to know the facts and attending circumstances which he reports; that he is accurate; and that he is honest. For not all contemporary writers are equally trustworthy, and the historian must weigh the testimony of each and all. Eye-witnesses are to be preferred. In using contemporary accounts one must always discriminate between the passages where writers speak as eye-witnesses and those where they repeat merely the testimony of others (p. 144). The testimony of intelligent contemporaries who are in agreement may be accepted when there is no reason to doubt it—when, in other words, they were in a position to know the truth and had no reason to conceal it (p. 150). It is when contemporary writers differ, or contradict one another, that the greatest care must be taken to evaluate their testimony.

This bald statement does scant justice to Père Griffet's clever exposition, for the little book abounds in examples drawn from many sources which bear witness to his own well-controlled technique. It is a shrewd intelligence that he brings to bear upon many historical problems; and many of his incidental observations are both keen and suggestive. Yet, with all his penetration, he was a child of the age—and of the church. His attitude toward the supernatural in human testimony is the outcome of the long conflict between historical criticism and theology, which year by year was becoming more intense. In a thoroughly modern spirit and with great practical sense he discusses such wonder-tales as that of Cleopatra's pearl; and of soothsayings and prophecies he remarks: "If you find in such sayings circumstances so detailed that it would have been impossible to foresee them, hold it for certain that they have been added after the occurrence to give the appearance of the miraculous to a very simple and natural fact." But then he adds, piously: "For, whatever one may say, there is no other means of knowing the future with exactitude but by an express, supernatural, and divine revelation. None of these alleged astrological predictions may be compared with the prophecies which we read in the Bible and which reason and religion oblige us to regard as true manifestations of the knowledge of God." One must not confound the wonders recounted by profane historians, he remarks in this same chapter, with miracles such as appear in lives of the saints, for these have a respectable purpose in view and are too well established to permit of doubt.

Not to leave Père Griffet in memory merely as a loyal supporter of established religion, I must add a single quotation from a passage in which with rare good sense he discusses the question whether the historian should spread the proof of his account before the reader's eyes: "L'historien a besoin de me dire les raisons qu'il a eues d'admettre ou de rejetter un tel fait, pour me persuader qu'il est faux ou véritable, lorsqu'il a lieu de croire que je dois être prévenu d'une opinion contraire à la sienne" (p. 371).

In these early attempts at formulation of historical method there is always the tacit assumption that, given accounts by contemporaries who both could and would tell the truth, the historian may attain certitude. The honest and intelligent witness is always assumed to be a faithful medium. None of these pioneers in methodology has any real insight into the psychology of perception and testimony. It was a German theologian and philosopher, Johann Martin Chladni, or Chladenius, to use the latinized form of his name, who was the first to attack the problem of certitude from the angle of psychology. Chladenius was not an historian but he was deeply concerned in historical problems by reason of the attacks on the historical foundations of Christianity; and the work which he published in 1752 with the title *Allgemeine Geschichtswissenschaft* was designed to set forth the intellectual processes by which historical knowledge is acquired, and to point out how, under control, these processes would lead, if not to certitude, at least to a high degree of historical probability. That his knowledge of psychological processes is faulty does not detract from the significance of his book, though it renders a fair summary in modern terms exceedingly difficult.

Chladenius sees clearly that the problem of perception is the fundamental problem in historical method. For every historical event there must be an observer. Every observer experiences sensations out of which he constructs representations (*Anschauungsurteile*). The human mind is no mere sensitive plate upon which the world of things is photographed—to express his idea in modern terms—but an active receiving agency. In perception, general concepts are brought to bear upon the sense-content. A constructive process goes on. The sense of sight, for example, reveals a sparkling stone: the intelligent observer says that he sees a diamond. Each mind reacts in its own way, according to its own habits. Every observer has a viewpoint which will vary with circumstances, physical or mental. The accounts of observers, therefore, will differ, often so widely as to seem contradictory. Not only this, but the viewpoint of the individual will alter his original sense impression (*Urbild*), so that in recollecting and narrating his experience he will compress and condense the details furnished by the senses. Language itself aids this testimonial process by supplying words that sum up details, just as a figure of speech may convey a series of impressions. And, so, personal feelings and motives are bound to enter into a recital of facts, subtly changing the details or altering the emphasis, all without any ill-will or perfidy upon the part of the narrator. Chladenius holds, therefore, that there can be no such thing as an impartial recital of events: "Eine unparteiische Erzählung kann nicht soviel heissen, als eine Sache ohne allen Sehepunkt erzählen, denn das ist einmal nicht möglich."

Further changes take place as a tale passes from the original observer to a second and third narrator. A series of such persons Chladenius terms a channel of communication (*Kanal*). The tale repeated by any one in the series is necessarily less complete than it was in the beginning. It is at best an excerpt (*Auszug*). Besides, those who repeat a tale have different viewpoints and are likely to make conjectures where actual knowledge fails them. Consequently, in all cases, it is a matter of prime concern to know whether a tale comes from the original teller or observer (*Urheber* or *Zuschauer*), or is repeated by some one else (*Nachsager*). Errors may occur all along the line: errors of omission and errors of commission; wilful errors and stupid errors.

With these preliminaries Chladenius approaches the crux of his problem: How, in view of all these possible alternatives, can an historian arrive at certainty? His first answer is almost naïve: one must believe an original observer unless there is reason to doubt what he says. Why? Because man is by nature a reasonable and truthful creature. To lie is contrary to the nature of the soul. But what if the original observer is ill-informed or stupid? Chladenius replies that one must ascertain what the reputation of an observer is. If he is found to be an eye-witness of the events which he reports and both capable and honest, then his testimony will stand; if his reputation is not satisfactory, it must be "supplemented" (*ergänzet*), by an oath if possible, or if not by an oath, then by witnesses: "Hauptsächlich wird das Ansehen eines Aussagers durch Zeugen ergänzet."

Chladenius is none too confident of reaching certitude by human testimony; and he therefore points out at length how the historian may use, as evidential material, traces (*Spuren*) and remains (*Überbleibsel*), documentary material (*Schriften*), and memorials (*Denkmäle*). That such material must undergo critical examination, he is well aware, and he points out that auxiliary studies like philology and palæography must be laid under requisition; but on these rungs of the ladder, he is convinced, an historian may mount to historical certainty.

The rationalistic spirit which permeated French thought in the eighteenth century found a vulnerable mark in the traditional histories of the church and in the histories of Roman antiquities. The credulity of the former in all that concerned the lives of saints and the readiness of the latter to accept the myths and legends surrounding the beginnings of the Eternal City, brought all historical writing under suspicion and provoked a general scepticism regarding the certitude of history. It was this widespread scepticism that found expression in the cynical remark of Fontenelle that history is only a fable upon which men have agreed.[1] In this atmosphere constructive methodology did not thrive; and the only book between Griffet's *Traité* and the end of the century that makes any pretence at formulating rules of historical study bears the title *De la manière d'écrire l'histoire.*[2] It is written in the form of a dialogue and doubtless owed its popularity to its literary cleverness. It contributes nothing of importance to methods of research, but it reflects admirably the temper of the times, as, for example, when it puts these remarks into the mouth of the pedantic Eugenius: "Under pretence of stimulating the mind to virtue, by bringing proofs that Providence will not at any time desert it, he [the historian] must never call up the intervention of a miracle in its favor. . . . Let us leave secondary causes to their own line of action; and, without recurring to prodigies for the purpose of either adorning our narrative, or of explaining events, the causes of which we cannot trace, let us suffer mankind to pay obedience to those general laws which God established at the beginning of the world."

[1] *L'histoire n'est qu'une fable convenue.*

[2] It was written by Bonnot de Mably and published at Paris in 1782. An English translation was published at London in 1783.

In England rationalistic thought found an exponent in David Hume, at once philosopher and historian. It was midway in the century that he sought to give the *coup de grâce* to the miraculous in human history, by a digression in his *Essay Concerning Human Understanding.*[1] "There is not to be found in all history," he wrote, "any miracle attested by a sufficient number of men, of such unquestioned good-sense, education, and learning, as to secure us against all delusion in themselves; of such undoubted integrity, as to place them beyond all suspicion of any design to deceive others; of such credit and reputation in the eyes of mankind, as to have a great deal to lose in case of their being detected in any falsehood; and at the same time, attesting facts, performed in such a public manner, and in so celebrated a part of the world, as to render the detection unavoidable."

It is perhaps not too much to assume that Wolf's attempt to eliminate Homer as the traditional author of the great epics was an outcropping of this same eighteenth century scepticism. Certain it is that the great strides in historical method for half a century were made by

[1] "Of Miracles," Section X, in *Essay Concerning Human Understanding* (1748).

classical philologists on German soil. To them fell the task of rehabilitating the history of classical antiquity by rigorous textual criticism and the study of inscriptions. In this wise grew up a body of accepted canons in philology which revolutionized the study of Greek and Latin historical sources.

Meantime, several short manuals appeared in Germany which attempted with more or less success to define the scope of historical studies and to formulate rules of historical criticism. All agree that history must be based mainly on testimonial evidence, and all stress the desirability of securing contemporary testimony. Most of them, too, grasp the importance of remains as confirmatory evidence; but not one undertakes to discuss in any thorough-going fashion the nature of historical proof. Perhaps any such discussion is too much to expect from manuals which were in the main designed for readers and general students of history. In the history of methodology they deserve mention for what they have to say about the commonly accepted ways of historical research.[1]

[1] First in point of time is Friedrich Rühs, *Entwurf einer Propadeutik des historischen Studiums* (1811), a suggestive little manual. It is significant of the dearth of works on method that Rühs names only Bodin's *Methodus*, Du Fresnoy's *Méthode*, and Bolingbroke's *Letters on the*

It is characteristic of the contributions to methodology in the nineteenth century that proof beyond reasonable doubt rather than absolute certainty is made the goal of historical research. To this extent the destructive scepticism of the eighteenth century left its mark upon historical study. By not claiming so much, historians were likely in the end to win more ground. The most considerable contribution in the first part of the century was made by P. C. F. Daunou in the first volume of his *Cours d'études historiques*, published in 1842. The title hardly suggests the wide range of the book. The first chapter sweeps away at the outset any expectation that the would-be historian may attain mathematical certainty in research, or that he may fix a mathematical standard of probability. Historical research never reaches more than moral certainty, which, we are reminded, is after all no more and no less than the certainty by which we weigh and measure human conduct in every-day life. Daunou has travelled a long

Study and Use of History. Chladenius is mentioned in another connection. A *Lehrbuch der Geschichte zum Gebrauche in höheren Unterrichts-Anstalten*, by Ludwig Wachler (1816), went through several editions. In an *Entwurf einer Theorie der Geschichte* (1820), W. Wachsmuth made a serious effort to lay a sure basis for historical research. It is the most discriminating of these shorter manuals. The *Lehrbuch der historischen Propädeutik und Grundriss der allgemeinen Geschichte* (1830), by Friedrich Rehm, owes much to its predecessors and offers nothing that is new.

way since his fellow-countrymen, Du Fresnoy and Griffet, touched ever so lightly on the problem of the miraculous in human affairs. He declares flat-footedly—and makes the declaration the first of his forty-nine rules—that no weight of merely human testimony can ever counterbalance the extreme improbability of a real suspension of the constant laws of the universe. Yet he hastens to add that what is often reported as miraculous may be only the consequence of some physical law which is not understood. Then the story may be stripped of its supernatural characteristics and be admitted as testimonial evidence for what it is worth. Testimony which contains improbable details should be discarded; or should be admitted as evidence only when the witnesses to the fact are so many and so reliable, that their falsity would be more incredible than the testimony itself.

Popular tradition Daunou handles with less assurance. He defines tradition as a popular opinion regarding facts which is universally held by a folk but which rests upon no contemporary testimony and has indeed no other foundation than a persistent belief running through two generations.[1] If such a tradition has had an

[1] Daunou quotes from a definition by Fréret in his *Reflexions sur l'étude des ancientes histoires:* "Ces opinions populaires, en conséquence des-

appreciable influence upon history, it ought to be taken into account, but always in such a way as to lead to no misapprehension as to its evidential value. But a tradition having a miraculous or unusual (*insolite*) character should be rejected without discussion. Traditions are admissible as evidence only when they are very probable in themselves; and then they should be treated as merely probable. To this the modern critic could hardly take exception. But then follows a rule which seems to open the pages of history to almost any persistent tradition: "Un récit traditionnel ne doit être considéré comme certain que, lorsqu'étant intrinsèquement probable, il a de plus retenti durant plusieurs siècles chez divers peuples, et obtenu partout une pleine croyance." [1]

Daunou is the first scholar to recognize newspapers and periodicals as important sources of history; and he makes some sagacious observations on their use. From them, he urges, one may glean with tolerable accuracy many dates

quelles toute une nation est persuadée de la vérité des faits, sans en avoir d'autres preuves que sa persuasion même et celle des générations précédentes, et sans que cette persuasion soit fondée sur aucun témoignage contemporain, subsistant séparément de la tradition même." Daunou, *Cours d'études historiques*, I, p. 75.

[1] Daunou, *Cours d'études historiques*, I, p. 469.

and many details of news, if one will use journals that represent various interests and opinions. Journals of the government are reliable so far as official notices and the like are concerned, but deserve no credence when their reports of happenings are edited in the interest of the government, unless indeed these accounts are confirmed by other news-sheets which have been published and edited independently of the government.

In the years 1869 and 1870 there appeared in a religious publication at Paris a series of articles by P. Ch. de Smedt, a Bollandist, which were subsequently published with additions in book form with the title *Principes de la critique historique*. The author professed to write for young people who wished to study history by a strictly scientific method; but lest such a study should shake the foundations of their faith, he was at pains to point out the distinction between the history of dogma and the history of ecclesiastical tradition. With the history of dogma his book is not concerned. The dogma of the church rests upon an unshakeable foundation. It was transmitted by the founder through Holy Writ and instructions to the Apostles and is preserved as infallible truth by the church with divine assistance.[1] Ecclesiastical traditions, however, have nothing to do with dogma: they rest upon testimony which must be subjected to critical tests like human testimony in secular matters. There is no reason to suppose that in purely historical matters the church fathers have "un privilège de quasi-infallibilité, parfaitement inutile pour la mission qu'ils avaient à remplir." [2]

Within these prescribed limits, Father de Smedt is a wise guide. Particularly noteworthy is his handling of the problem of popular tradition, which Daunou left in such a fog of uncertainty. There are two ways of dealing with such traditions. Some historians have accepted the substance of popular traditions which lack confirmatory contemporary testimony, while discarding details that seem improbable. This is a fallacious procedure, De Smedt contends, because there is often no substantial basis for the popular belief at all. And he cites the amusing story told by Mabillon of a church in Spain which petitioned Pope Urban VIII for a grant of indulgences at the fête of St. Viar, whose body it claimed to possess. Inquiry brought out that the only evidence of the existence of St. Viar

[1] De Smedt, *Principes de la critique historique*, pp. 163–4.
[2] *Ibid.*, p. 180.

was a stone with the Roman letters S. VIAR. Scholars soon demonstrated to the satisfaction of all save the Spanish petitioners, that the stone did not cover the remains of a saint but recalled only a bit of Roman antiquity. When the missing letters of the inscription were supplied, it read PRAEFECTU*S VIAR*UM.[1]

Other historians have dealt with the problem by using the argument from silence; that is, they have assumed that the absence of contradictory testimony is ground for believing a popular tradition. Father de Smedt insists that this argument must be used with all possible circumspection. Three conditions are usually attached: first, the main content of the tradition must be known publicly to many witnesses; second, it must have commanded assent for a very considerable length of time; third, it must have encountered no protest during this time even from those who would have had an interest in contradicting the story. Even with these conditions attached, the rule should be viewed with suspicion. The story of "la Papesse Jeanne," current down to the sixteenth century, complied with all these conditions, and yet it has been proved false in every particular. If

[1] Mabillon, *Iter italicum* (1724), p. 143. Cited by De Smedt, p. 193.

employed at all, the argument from silence should be subjected to two further conditions: first, the persons who might have contradicted the current tradition must have lived in an age when the critical sense was considerably developed; and second, these persons must have possessed the means to ascertain the truth. Even so, no more than a high degree of probability may be conceded to the tradition.[1] Had earlier ecclesiastical historians possessed Father de Smedt's habitual caution, the sceptical spirit of the eighteenth century would have had less to feed upon.

Some years before De Smedt's articles appeared, Joh. Gustav Droysen had been putting into the hands of his students at the University of Berlin a privately printed abstract of lectures

[1] In a slender pamphlet of thirty pages, with the title *Notions élémentaires de critique historique* (1883), Ad. Tardif remarks: "La tradition occupe un rang secondaire dans les sources historiques et elle ne peut suffire seule à établir la vérité d'un fait" (p. 17). He concludes nevertheless that tradition should be taken into account under the following conditions:

"Quand elle s'applique à un fait important et public, qui a eu nécessairement un grand nombre de témoins.

"Quand elle a été universellement admise pendant un laps de temps considérable.

"Quand elle n'a soulevé aucune objection de la part de personnes ayant intérêt à la contredire et disposant des moyens d'information nécessaires pour s'assurer de la réalité des faits."

There are some capital observations in this little pamphlet, though they need elaboration.

on "Historische Encyclopaedie und Methodologie," which with some additions he published in 1867, under the title *Grundriss der Historik.* Droysen is the logical successor of Chladenius; and he must be accounted the first writer on method to lay a sound philosophical basis for historical research. His terse, compact sentences are saturated with Kantian philosophy, to be sure, and his somewhat dogmatic assertions need at times important qualifications; but the fundamental principles of historical study are stated with great clarity.

The argument of the *Grundriss* runs in this wise: The science of history is the product of empirical observation, experience, and research. All empirical knowledge rests upon "the specific energy" of the sensory nerves, through the excitation of which the mind receives not copies (*Abbilder*), but symbols, of the outside world (*Zeichen von den Dingen draussen.*)[1] Hence it follows that the data of historical research are not past events (*Vergangenheiten*), for these have gone, but tokens of the past which may be retained by memory or be perceived as remains of

[1] Droysen presses far beyond Kant in saying that *Zeichen* correspond to *Dinge draussen*. How can he know? Of course, the most fundamental problem of philosophy is implicit in this statement.

what has been. So it is that the best sources give the investigator "only polarized light," so to speak. Historical criticism cannot reach the real historical fact, for the so-called historical fact is a complex of acts of the human will (p. 16). These acts have been performed; they are gone forever; they cannot be recalled. What remain are only traces (*Überreste*), representations (*Auffassungen*), memories. The most that historical criticism can do, therefore, is so to deal with this material as to make possible a comparatively true representation of historical facts (p. 19). In the light of these principles the *Grundriss* touches in quick succession upon the specific problems of criticism, interpretation, and presentation.

The first impression that Droysen must have made upon his student hearers was the futility of trying to know the past. His words and phrases have an almost forbidding sound. He speaks of "the ghostly presence of past events," of the empty darkness of the past, of the existence of only the Here and the Now. But he reassures his hearers by the reflection that, after all, the joy and the reward of historical research consist in the illuminating and revivifying light which the ingenious human mind may cast into the dark corners of the past. What Droysen brought into sharp relief—and it was no slight service—was the psychological conditions under which the historian must work. If history be a science, it is a peculiar sort of science which has little in common with those that rest on direct observation and that attain relative certainty by repeated experimentation.[1]

It is somewhat singular that no treatise on historical method was produced in England during the nineteenth century. English scholars have always preferred to work by rule of thumb and have consistently expressed some contempt for methodology. The only English book that deals with historical method, so far as my knowledge goes, is Sir George C. Lewis's *Treatise on the Methods of Observation and Reasoning in Politics*, published in 1852. In it there is a single chapter—the seventh—devoted to history. Lewis owes much to Daunou and his French predecessors, and he propounds little that is new or original, except possibly a rather forced analogy between tradition and "hearsay" as it was understood in English courts of justice.

To this same period belongs H. von Sybel's brochure *Über die Gesetze des historischen Wissens* (1864), which in its narrow compass contains the essence of historical criticism, written by a master who has deduced theory from practice.

Three years later appeared his *Inquiry into the Credibility of the Early Roman History*, in which he proposed to test the sources to see if and how far they were supported by the testimony of credible witnesses. Lewis protests that historical evidence does not differ in nature from other sorts. "Historical evidence, like judicial evidence, is founded on the testimony of credible witnesses. Unless these witnesses had personal and immediate perception of the facts which they report, unless they saw and heard what they undertake to relate as having happened, their evidence is not entitled to credit. As all original witnesses must be contemporary with the events which they attest, it is a necessary condition for the credibility of a witness that he be a contemporary; though a contemporary is not necessarily a credible witness." [1] Measured by this strict test of contemporaneousness, early Roman history down to the war with Pyrrhus was not authentic history at all, but only tradition. Few writers on method take so strict a view of contemporaneousness.[2]

[1] *Inquiry*, I, p. 16.

[2] The brochure printed by F. H. Bradley in 1874 on *The Presuppositions of Critical History* deserves mention, not because it contributes anything of importance to method, but because it discusses the nature of historical testimony and touches on the fundamental postulates of historical thinking. The study was occasioned, it would appear, by the

The time was now ripe for a systematic manual on historical method, for a treatise which should gather up and put in pragmatical form the approved modes of procedure in historical criticism as they had been put forward and elucidated by historical thinkers from Mabillon to Droysen. This great service was rendered by Ernst Bernheim, in his *Lehrbuch der historischen Methode*, published in 1889.[1] His distinct contribution to methodology consists in his sharp definition of the problems of historical research and in his illustrations, drawn from extraordinarily varied sources, of the ways and means of reaching their solution. He has lifted methodology from a loose collection of platitudes and haphazard rules to a self-conscious discipline with a highly developed technique. He has codified rather than created, but his service is not less real because he has refrained from breaking new ground. To review

critical work of Baur and his school, and Bradley is chiefly interested in the question whether historical testimony can establish "the non-analogous." To this—to him—crucial question, he returns again and again. Had he chosen to follow up this first essay by an extended examination of the principles of historical evidence, the literature of historical methodology would have been by so much the richer; but in that case his fellow-philosophers would perhaps never have seen his *Appearance and Reality* and other metaphysical essays.

[1] This *Lehrbuch* was revised and enlarged in 1894; again revised and enlarged in 1903, with the words *Und der Geschichtsphilosophie* added to the title; and since then twice reprinted without alterations.

his book in detail would be to recapitulate what has already been said on the technique of historical criticism and the assessment of evidence.[1] Bernheim stands almost at the end of a long development. Few studies now possess a more complete technique than history, taking the cognate humanistic subjects like philology and palæography into consideration. The defect of the *Lehrbuch*—if defect it is in a book dealing chiefly with historical criticism—is its lack of adequate discussion of the nature of historical proof, the summation of evidence.

Since Bernheim first published his *Lehrbuch*, various manuals have appeared, nearly all of which flatter him by imitation. Exception may be made of the *Introduction aux études historiques*, by Langlois and Seignobos, which, within its small compass, contains not only excellent advice to students but some important considerations on evidence that escaped Bernheim's attention.[2] In Germany, Spain, and Italy manuals have appeared from time to time which follow Bernheim closely. The *Lehrbuch der geschichtlichen Methode*, by Alfred Feder, makes no advance beyond

[1] See chapters III and IV.

[2] This *Introduction*, published in 1898, was translated immediately into English and published in London in the same year.

Bernheim—is, indeed, in many respects reactionary in its point of view, especially in matters concerning ecclesiastical history and tradition. It has found favor with Catholic students, however, and has reached a third edition (1924). In the United States, Professor F. M. Fling has done much to direct the attention of historical scholars to problems of method both by papers contributed to historical journals and by two small volumes bearing the titles *Outline of Historical Method* (1899) and *The Writing of History* (1920). It is doubtful if the author of *Historical Evidence* (1909)—H. B. George—understands fully the purport of his title. He shows no familiarity with "the elaborate books on historical method in various languages," to which he alludes in his preface, and he refers to the *Introduction* of Langlois and Seignobos only to misquote it on a fundamental point—the credibility of the unsupported testimony of a single witness (p. 98). The book contains some wise counsel to beginners, however, and may serve its purpose as an introductory manual.

Professor John Martin Vincent in his *Historical Research*, published in 1911, has tried to supply the lack of an adequate manual in English. It is avowedly an outline rather than a thorough-going treatise after the Teutonic fashion, yet it contains matter which one will look for elsewhere in vain, even in the heavily weighted pages of Bernheim. The chapter on the newspaper as a source of history is of particular suggestiveness to American students. Had Professor Vincent seen fit to expand and elaborate his chapter on the nature of historical evidence, he would have anticipated many pages in this book.

The history of historical method suggests the need of examining more carefully the nature of historical proof, for, however carefully the historical critic may prune and trim his sources, he must sooner or later sum up his evidence and ask what and how much it proves. Historical proof is something more than the mere arithmetical sum of authorities, and it rests upon postulates which have been too readily taken for granted.

CHAPTER VI

THE NATURE OF HISTORICAL PROOF

To say that a historian should tell the truth is a counsel of perfection. It assumes that there is absolute truth to which he may attain. Such a quest, however, is as hopeless as the metaphysician's search after "things-in-themselves"—that hypothetical outside world of things which are supposed to stimulate our sense-organs to activity. The most that philosophers can know is the world as given in consciousness; and the most that historians can know is that historical past which has been perceived and reported by human intelligence. The history of the world is the history of the world as constructed in human consciousness under distinct limitations. Whether the historian's aim is to tell "how it really was" or "how it really came to be," he can never reach mathematical certainty, and he is fortunate indeed if he can reach a high degree of probability, a probability beyond reasonable doubt. There is an inevitable relativity in historiography.

The problem thus raised has already been foreshadowed in an earlier chapter.[1] Given the limitations of human perception and memory, and the fallibility of human testimony, how can any certain knowledge of the past be gained? It is this problem in one form or another that has troubled all writers on historical method from Bodin to Bernheim. Let us state the problem more simply and concretely: granting to an eyewitness an unexceptionable character and the most favorable conditions for making his observations, dare we say that his testimony establishes the historical reality of the facts reported —that his facts are "true" facts?

Bernheim does not solve the problem satisfactorily. A judgment of reliability, he insists, rests upon the accepted axiom that no man will without purpose or cause misrepresent the facts which he knows.[2] In an authentic piece of testimony we are justified in holding the recorded facts as true when nothing can be found in the

[1] Chapter II. "The Basis of Historical Doubt."

[2] Kein Mensch pflegt die Thatsachen, welche er weiss, ohne Grund und Zweck falsch mitzuteilen." Bernheim, *Lehrbuch*, p. 404. De Smedt states the axiom as follows: "L'homme a une inclination naturelle à reconnaître et à affirmer la vérité, et il ne se laissera aller à l'erreur et surtout à l'imposture que lorsq'il y sera poussé par des affections ou des intérêts assez puissants pour entraîner la volonté libre en sens contraire." *Principes de la critique historique*, p. 61.

character of the witness, or in his mental make-up, or in his position, that would cause misrepresentation (*Entstellung*).[1] In other words, the absence of dishonesty or any pathological symptoms in a witness is ground for holding his testimony to be true. This is really begging the question, for the fundamental question is not the honesty of the witness but the accuracy of his perceptions. It is a faulty psychology which assumes that a normal healthy person can never make a mistake. And Bernheim himself immediately qualifies his statement by adding: "After all, it is only a negative judgment." We can only say of a witness: nothing has been found out to his disadvantage. There may still be reasons for misrepresentation which we have not discovered. "A final verdict on the reality of events cannot be reached by considering merely the reliability of a witness." [2] But then, as though alarmed at the far-reaching consequences of this admission, Bernheim lames the force of his conclusion by

[1] Bernheim, *opus cit.*, p. 359

[2] Bernheim, *opus cit.*, p. 359. Feder, in his *Lehrbuch der geschichtlichen Methode*, repeats the aphorism *nemo gratis mendax* over and over again, as though the absence of a motive for dishonesty removed all doubt as to the perceptive capacity of a witness; for example, pp. 27, 254 ff. Yet elsewhere he seems to admit that even in the case of normal moral beings variation from the truth may occur without their knowledge or intent. See *opus cit.*, p. 213.

adding: "Accounts of events which are so simple, so neutral, and, I might say, so monumental in character, that the witness could not have been either deceived or mistaken, and in which no motive for misrepresentation is apparent, we may take for certain; and such accounts have indeed never been rejected." Just what these simple, neutral, and monumental events are, we are not told. It would be interesting to know how Bernheim ascertains that events are monumental, when they are reported only by this simple witness; and how events can be so simple and neutral that an observer could not be at fault. For my part I cannot conceive of events so simple that they could not be falsely reported.

Charles Seignobos takes sharp issue with Bernheim on this crucial matter.[1] "It is a principle common to all sciences of observation," he writes, "not to base a scientific conclusion on a single observation; the fact must have been corroborated by several independent observations before it can be affirmed. History, with its imperfect modes of acquiring information, has less right than any other science to claim exemption from this principle. An historical statement is,

[1] *Introduction aux études historiques.* This book is the joint work of Ch. V. Langlois and Ch. Seignobos.

in the most favorable case, only an indifferently made observation; it needs other observations to corroborate it."[1] And again: "An isolated observation is not admitted into science: it is quoted (with the observer's name), but no conclusions are drawn from it. Historians have no avowable motive for proceding otherwise."[2]

There is one other condition under which Bernheim is disposed to give probative value to the testimony of a single unexceptionable witness. If such testimony is supported by "inner probability," it may be admitted as having complete evidential value. Inner probability seems to mean, if I read the context of Bernheim's brief statement aright, compatibility with a series of events otherwise fully attested, or conformity with a general trend of events known through other sources.[3] Seignobos admits the validity of this form of proof, using the phrase "harmony of the facts." "Several facts which, taken in isolation, are only imperfectly proved, may confirm each other in such a manner as to produce a collective certainty."[4]

[1] *Opus cit.*, p. 167.
[2] *Opus cit.*, p. 169.
[3] Bernheim's phrase is: Ubereinstimmung eines Quellenzeugnisses mit dem uns sonst bekannten allgemeinen Zusammenhang der Thatsachen. *Lehrbuch,* p. 368.
[4] Langlois et Seignobos, *Introduction,* p. 173.

This sort of proof is valid, however, only under one imperious condition, which neither Bernheim nor Seignobos states with sufficient definiteness. Only when all other possibilities are excluded as inconsistent, incompatible, out of harmony with the chain of events or facts, can the testimony in question be regarded as having high probative value. Not any and every piece of testimony that seems to fit may be regarded as proved by inner probability, but only such testimony as survives in competition with all other possibilities. The logical rule that applies is simple enough: an inference is valid only when it is a necessary inference—when all other possible inferences have been excluded as logically impossible.

What shall be said of the probative value of testimony by two or more witnesses? In everyday life we believe a story vouched for by two persons whose word we trust, if we are assured that they got their information independently of each other. But if two persons should tell exactly the same story, using precisely the same phrases and following precisely the same order in narrative details, we should at once suspect some collusion. The tacit postulate from which we argue is, that two men quite independently would not happen upon the same facts and describe them in exactly the same way. This is a sound enough rule for practical conduct; but the historian must add a further qualification. Two witnesses might tell a plausible tale when in fact both had been misled or deceived by a common cause. Two eye-witnesses of a battle might report an episode in substantially the same way, and wrongly, because they had both stood on the same spot, where only a partial view of the field was possible. Partisanship or some strong emotional bias might deflect the testimony of two witnesses so as to produce a general agreement which would be false to the facts. These considerations have led a German scholar[1] to formulate a widely accepted rule, which reads as follows: "When two or more contemporary (eye and ear) witnesses report *independently of one another* the same fact with many like details that do not have a necessary or usual but rather a casual connection with the fact, then the accounts, so far as they agree, must be true, *if the fact and its details were so clearly perceptible that no self-deception could have been possible.*"

If all these conditions could be fulfilled—if

[1] Adolf Rhomberg, *Die Erhebung der Geschichte zum Range einer Wissenschaft* (1883).

a historian could always be sure that two witnesses had gained their information independently and were not victims of self-deception or perceptual errors—then, indeed, history would attain a high degree of probability, if not certainty. But every serious investigator knows that these conditions are almost never completely fulfilled. In every honest mind there will remain a lingering shadow of doubt about the details of events which are known only by the testimony of remote individuals who can never be interrogated or subjected to cross-examination. The possibilities of error can never be entirely removed. Hence the need of securing corroborative evidence wherever possible, such as public documentary material and the mute testimony of remains of unimpeachable authenticity.[1]

To bring into sharp relief the peculiar nature of historical proof, I have chosen a common but subtle type of evidential material, the testimony of eye-witnesses of a series of stirring events. The personal, anecdotal, dramatic moments of

[1] It is rather extraordinary that in a book written by such scholars as Langlois and Seignobos, only documents should be considered, by which they mean written or printed documents. There is a single reference to remains on page 45. "On peut distinguer deux espèces de documents. Parfois le fait passé a laissé une trace matérielle (un monument, un objet fabriqué)." But no attempt is made to explain the important evidential value of such material.

history are precisely those that test critical acumen most severely. Happily, the historian is not dependent upon such material alone. A great part of history must be written from those public records which may be regarded as composite testimony. The acts of legislative bodies, executive documents, decisions of courts of law, reports of commissions, treaties, diplomatic papers, official correspondence, public documents in general, so far as they state facts of record, are a sort of resultant of many acts of will, a deposit left by conflicting currents of thought, a product of many minds. Neither their authenticity nor their testimony as to public facts can be impeached, though their motivation may be variously explained. It is against this fairly stable background that testimony as to events must be weighed and measured. And it is in this connection that proof by harmony of facts may be used legitimately. If, for example, the general orders issued to a commander of military forces on the eve of a battle are preserved in the archives of a ministry of war, as well as his detailed orders to subordinate officers before and during the engagement, then the testimony of an eye-witness of the military operations, which would otherwise have little value, may be fitted into the trend of events and so receive emphatic corroboration.[1]

Throughout these pages—throughout all histories and manuals of historical method—runs the tacit postulate that an historian may enter into the thoughts and feelings of men of other times. Von Sybel insists, in a pamphlet *On the Laws of Historical Knowledge*,[2] that it is possible to penetrate to the inmost being of another person, to note the genesis of his perceptions, and to take the measure of his very concepts and feelings. In a qualified sense, this may be true; but if so, it is only because of the identity of human nature in all times and places. This identity is, indeed, a postulate of all historical thinking. Every historian works on the principle of analogy which predicates like attributes and like functions of human nature wherever found.[3]

[1] "The critic always endeavors to go back to the first source and, so far as possible, to draw his information not from narratives, but from such documents as have been part of the episode under investigation—not from the account of a battle by a general, for example, but from his orders before and during the battle." H. von Sybel, "Gedächtnisrede auf Leopold von Ranke," in *Historische Zeitschrift* for 1886, pp. 474–5.

[2] H. von Sybel, *Über die Gesetze des historischen Wissens* (1864).

[3] "Die Identität der Menschennatur ist die Grundaxiom jeder historischen Erkenntnis." Bernheim, *Lehrbuch*, p. 192.

"On suppose que les êtres, objets, actes, motifs, qu'on n'a pas pu observer, mais qu'on connaît indirectement par les documents, sont ana-

Is this a reasonable postulate? Considering merely the matter of feeling and emotion, may we predicate of Ethiopians in the days of Herodotus, of Persians in the time of Cyrus, of Greeks at the siege of Troy, of Hindus in the reign of Akbar, of Chinese in the age of Confucius, the same emotional response as of the mountain-folk of Tennessee and the university men of the British Isles? If we were to judge by behavioristic responses alone, we could hardly escape the conclusion that the differences between men of varying cultural stages are more obvious than the resemblances. The abhorrence which the modern man feels at the ruthless slaughter of prisoners of war is a feeling that primitive man never manifested. We revolt at the thought of cannibalism; but the South Sea islander developed a relish for human flesh. The Greek hero shed tears of rage or joy under emotional stress; the modern hero prides himself on his self-control under all circumstances. Helpless aged Hindus sought Nirvana under the wheels of

logues à ceux qu'on connaît par l'observation du monde actuel. C'est le postulat nécessaire à toutes les sciences documentaires: si les faits rapportés par les documents n'avaient pas été analogues à ceux que nous observons, nous n'y pourrions rien comprendre." Seignobos, *La Méthode historique appliquée aux sciences sociales*, p. 120.

"La méthode historique est exclusivement une méthode d'interpretation psychologique par analogie." *Ibid.*, p. 25.

the Juggernaut; infirm old men and women in America find relative consolation and comfort in homes for the aged. Ancient peoples sought to escape the miseries of over-population by infanticide; we establish day-nurseries and foundling asylums.

That modern conditions demand infinitely more delicate adjustments on the part of man than in earlier times, can hardly be denied. And, in all probability, men have developed a far greater sensitivity than at any previous stage in societal evolution. Hence mere quantitative differences in reactions to environment seem to point to a qualitative difference in human beings on different levels of culture.

Over against this argument must be set the quick response of the modern man to the play and interplay of elemental human instincts as they appear in one form or another in ancient literature. How can we account for the perennial appeal of the Homeric poems and the Athenian drama, except upon the assumption that human nature has remained fundamentally, if not superficially, the same? The capacity of the modern man to appreciate the ethical values of the tenets of Confucius, the sayings of Jesus, and the meditations of Marcus Aurelius, argues a nature that can evaluate abstract goodness in whatever form it may be clothed. A play depicting the elemental passions of Tennessee mountain-folk has held London audiences spell-bound and moved phlegmatic Englishmen to tears. The argument can also be carried into the realm of æsthetics, where we are often most acutely conscious of varying standards and tastes. The perfection of Greek sculpture, whatever it owed to time and place, was essentially an achievement of the human spirit, and it has not lost in these twenty centuries its appeal to the beauty-loving instinct in men.

It may well be that, far back of recorded time, the ancestors of man possessed such rudimentary intelligence that they seemed nearer the brute than the modern man; but with them the historian has no concern. In the absence of records and remains there is no history. It is man possessing the power of articulate speech and the ability to record his activities who is the subject of history. And there is no good reason to suppose that, in the short space of time which we call history, any appreciable change has occurred in human instincts or in those conscious processes by which knowledge is acquired, however much affective states of consciousness may have increased in intensity and duration. For the purpose of weighing evidence the historical scholar demands of his authorities only the fundamental powers of mind which the older logicians described as the power of discrimination, the power of detecting identity, and the power of retention.[1]

In common with the physical sciences, history postulates also the uniformity of nature; that is, a universe in which similar causes are followed by similar effects. The historian assumes that the recorder of ancient happenings faced a physical universe identical with his own. He extends his consciousness,[2] so to speak, to include that of an ancient writer partly because—as has been said—he assumes an identity of human nature, and also because he believes that ancient writers beheld only physical phenomena which were like those within his own experience. Herodotus records the story of the circumnavigation of Africa by the Phœnicians but expresses his disbelief, because such an exploit was without analogy in the astronomical world that he knew.[3]

Another postulate implicit in much historical writing is that expressed in the phrase "con-

[1] W. Stanley Jevons, *The Principles of Science: A Treatise on Logic and Scientific Method* (2d. Ed., 1877), pp. 4–5.

[2] The phrase is Bradley's. *Opus cit.*, p. 23.

[3] Herodotus, IV, 42.

tinuity of history." It stands in sharp contradistinction to the old postulate, which found so ready an expositor in Bossuet, that an all-wise and omnipotent Providence governs the affairs of men, intervening in His good will and pleasure in the ongoings of life on earth. Instead of being a pawn in a game, man is conceived now as an organism adjusting itself to an environment by instinct or intelligence. In the broadest sense, history is mankind adjusting itself continuously to the physical universe. Into this notion has crept also the idea of progress, fortified by the evolutionary hypothesis, so that this process of adjustment is conceived as a movement toward a goal, that goal being rather vaguely visualized as a perfect order of society.

It is unfortunate that such a concept as this, which has inspired so much excellent research in history, should be termed a *law* of human progress, for law carries with it the implication of an immutable and prescribed rule, and this concept is no more than an abstraction, a product of thought. There is nothing which imposes this concept of the continuity of history upon us except the experience that empirically it explains a great many happenings. That it may be displaced by another "law," is well within the range of possibility. After all, as Ernest Mach has so well said, the so-called laws of nature are in their origin only limitations which experience teaches us to apply to our expectations.[1]

[1] "Ihrem Ursprung nach sind die 'Naturgesetze' Einschränkungen, die wir unter Leitung der Erfahrung unserer Erwartung vorschreiben." Ernest Mach, *Erkenntnis und Irrtum*, p. 449.

CHAPTER VII

THE USE OF HYPOTHESES

Although historians have borrowed many scientific methods, they have shown an odd reluctance to resort openly to the use of hypotheses. To many, an hypothesis has seemed like a commitment, a pre-judgment, when the mind should be kept open for the observation of facts. History, say they, should be studied without prejudices or prepossessions. And many would assent unreservedly to the advice of Francis Bacon, that "men should bid themselves for a while renounce conceptions and begin to make acquaintance with things themselves." [1] It is interesting to note, however, that Bacon did not follow his own advice and that modern scientists have ignored his caveat.[2] "Nature gives no reply to a general inquiry," remarks Sir E. R. Lankester; "she must be interrogated by questions

[1] This would seem to be the view of J. B. Bury, whose practice is much better than his theory. "This work," he writes, "this hewing of wood and drawing of water, has to be done in faith—in the faith that a complete assemblage of the smallest facts of human history will tell in the end." *An Inaugural Lecture* (1903), p. 31. For this and the following quotations I am indebted to F. J. Teggart's suggestive *Prolegomena to History*, chap. II, "The Method of Science."

[2] W. S. Jevons, *The Principles of Science*, pp. 506–7.

which already contain the answer she is to give; in other words, the observer can only observe that which he is led by hypothesis to look for."[1] The testimony of Charles Darwin is to the same effect: "About thirty years ago there was much talk that geologists ought to observe and not theorize; and I well remember some one saying that at this rate a man might as well go into a gravel-pit and count the pebbles and describe the colors. How odd it is that any one should not see that all observation must be for or against some view if it is to be of any service."[2] And Huxley takes the same point of view in no uncertain fashion: "It is a favorite popular delusion that the scientific inquirer is under a sort of moral obligation to abstain from going beyond that generalization of observed facts which is absurdly called Baconian induction. But any one who is practically acquainted with scientific work is aware that those who refuse to go beyond fact, rarely get as far as fact; and any one who has studied the history of science knows that almost every great step therein has been made by the 'anticipation of Nature,' that is, by the invention of hypotheses, which, though verifiable,

[1] Sir E. R. Lankester, *The Advancement of Science* (1890), p. 9.
[2] Charles Darwin, *More Letters*, ed. by Francis Darwin (1903), I, p. 195.

often had very little foundation to start with; and, not infrequently, in spite of a long career of usefulness, turned out to be wholly erroneous in the long run."[1]

To all this historians reply: "It is different with history." The sciences of direct observation, like physics, chemistry, and biology, they would contend, are neutral in tone; they do not appeal to any prejudices, inherited or acquired from every-day life. A chemist does not look at a test-tube with the eyes of a Whig or with the eyes of a Tory, as Baptist or Methodist, as Protectionist or Free Trader. An historian, however, must deal with the very stuff out of which daily life is made, its follies, its superstitions, its theories, its practices, its ideals. The more reason, therefore, why he should divest himself of prejudices and predilections, so far as he can, and approach his material with open mind and a desire only to know what the facts teach.

Admirable as this attitude is in theory, it is psychologically untenable. Open-minded, of course, every investigator should be; but open-mindedness does not mean mental vacuity. No active intelligence can be totally devoid of

[1] T. H. Huxley, "The Progress of Science" (1887), in *Collected Essays*, vol. I, p. 62.

general ideas nor divest itself of accumulated experiences. A mind devoid of prepossessions is likely to be devoid of all mental furniture. And the historian who thinks that he can clean his mind as he would a slate with a wet sponge, is ignorant of the simplest facts of mental life. "The objectivity on which some of them pride themselves," remarks a caustic critic, "will (centuries hence) be looked upon not as freedom from, but as unconsciousness on their part of, the preconceived notions which have governed them." [1]

What historians distrust, however, is really not hypotheses that invite investigation—fluid hypotheses, if one may use the term—but fixed theories that control investigation. The literature of history is strewn with examples of such ruling theories. In our own day, the great fertility of economic studies has bred a type of historian that has pushed determinism to the extreme limit. Not content with interpreting the general drift of social groups in terms of economic interests—a legitimate and often profitable undertaking—they have attempted to impose their theory rigorously and to explain

[1] J. T. Merz, *A History of European Thought in the Nineteenth Century* (1896), I, p. 7.

individual behavior in the same terms, often ignoring important data which do violence to the theory. Not only this; they have sometimes forced the facts to fit the theory.

Some of the recent studies of sectionalism in American history exemplify the danger of a ruling theory. Succinctly stated, the general theory assumes that well-defined physiographic areas will tend to produce distinct sets of economic interests, which, in the long run, will find expression in policy. The physiographic region becomes an economic section with political potentialities. If, then, the political demands of a section become articulate and express themselves in the choice of congressmen, for example, the historian points back to economic interests as the "cause" of the phenomena of politics. It is an engaging theory, which has explained many obscure phases of American politics, but there is a subtle fallacy in much of this reasoning.

The method used to demonstrate the influence of sectionalism is to plot election returns by counties or congressional districts, assigning to Whigs or to Democrats, to Native Americans or to Republicans, this or that constituency according as it elected a Whig, or a Democrat, a Native American or a Republican. In many of these tabulations, no account is taken of opposing election returns, which are often only slightly less than a majority through a period of years. The tabulator has taken only the majority vote of a district and then has recorded the vote in Congress of the representative chosen by that majority. Can it be affirmed confidently that physiographic conditions controlled the political action of a district of two hundred thousand voters when ninety-nine thousand were in opposition? The action of such factors as climate, soil, distribution of population ought to be fairly constant and uniform on most of the inhabitants of a physiographical section.

It is probable, as Venn pointed out, that the scientific hypothesis had its origin in the conditions and necessities of primitive life, in "that very familiar state of things in our practical life in which we are in doubt between two or more alternatives"—a situation which gave occasion for "the use of the particle 'if': in other words, for the use of the hypothetical proposition." [1] The process consists essentially in making suppositions, in entertaining concepts or mental pictures, in the hope that one alternative or

[1] J. Venn, *The Principles of Empirical or Inductive Logic*, p. 388.

another will turn out to be "true."[1] The scientific hypothesis, however, is more than a guess. "It is a preliminary tentative supposition for the better understanding of facts which, however, as yet eludes actual proof."[2] In formulating a hypothesis we try to take into account the properties of a fact as our observation under limited circumstances has revealed them, without knowing whether these properties will appear under other, more general, conditions—without knowing, in short, whether the hypothesis will fit and how far it will reach, under these conditions.[3] In its origin at least, an hypothesis is not a prepossession which commits the maker to a judgment of facts. It is a mental attitude, "the attitude, to wit, of *inventing* a mental content, of *holding it in suspense*, of taking it as a possibility, not as an assured fact, of assuming it experimentally for the argument's sake and in order to test its value by its consequences."[4] So far from assuring a definite result, an hypothesis may prove unsatisfactory and be discarded. Physical

[1] M. C. Ashley, "The Nature of Hypothesis" in Dewey's *Studies in Logical Theory*.

[2] E. Mach. *Erkenntnis und Irrtum*, p. 235.

[3] I have paraphrased the suggestive remarks of Mach, on page 243 of his *Erkenntnis und Irrtum*.

[4] F. C. S. Schiller on "Hypothesis" in Singer's *Studies in the History and Method of Science*, II, p. 416.

science has made progress only by trying and rejecting hypotheses.[1] The hypothesis that successfully holds the field in this competition is the one accepted by the experimenter as provisionally true. It is so accepted, not because it conforms to some immutable external standard of truth, but because it works best—explains most satisfactorily the body of facts under examination.[2]

It can hardly be denied, however, that there is a subtle tendency to bestow a sort of parental affection upon an intellectual offspring—to yield "to the partiality of paternalism." [3] And if this influence is not resolutely offset, the use-

[1] "Very lame and imperfect theories are sufficient to suggest useful experiments, which serve to correct those theories, and give birth to others more perfect. These then occasion farther experiments, which bring us still nearer to the truth, and in this method of approximation, we must be content to proceed, and we ought to think ourselves happy, if, in this slow method, we make any real progress." J. Priestley, *History and Present State of Discoveries Relating to Vision, Light, and Colors* (1772), I, p. 181. Commenting on the discovery of new truth, Whewell remarks: "It commonly succeeds by guessing; and this success seems to consist in framing several tentative hypotheses and selecting the right one." *Novum Organon Renovatum*, p. 59.

[2] Schiller, as a pragmatist, expresses great impatience with logicians who use the expressions "true hypotheses" and "right hypotheses." "No verification," he insists, "will ever prove more than that the observations are compatible with the hypotheses they test." "The sole essential of a scientific hypothesis is that it should *work*—relevantly of course to the problems of the science." *Opus cit.*, pp. 442–444.

[3] The figure of speech is T. C. Chamberlin's. See his article on "The Method of Multiple Working Hypotheses," in *Science*, vol. 15 (1890).

fulness of an hypothesis vanishes. As a means of control Professor T. C. Chamberlin has urged the use of multiple hypotheses. "The effort is to bring into view every rational explanation of new phenomena and to develop every tenable hypothesis respecting their cause and history. The investigator thus becomes the parent of a family of hypotheses; and, by his parental relation to all, he is forbidden to fasten his affections unduly upon any one." [1]

Some advantages undoubtedly are gained by formulating several hypotheses. It may be true in science that a single hypothesis predisposes the investigator to favor a single explanatory conception when an adequate explanation involves the co-ordination of several factors. In that case multiple hypotheses may promote more thorough investigation; and the reaction of one upon another may, as Chamberlin says, "amplify the recognized scope of each" and so "whet the discriminative edge of each." "Each hypothesis suggests its own criteria, its own means of proof, its own methods of developing the truth; and if a group of hypotheses compass the subject on all sides, the total outcome of means and methods is full and rich." [2]

[1] *Ibid.*, p. 93.

[2] *Opus cit.*, p. 94.

It is not so clear that the use of multiple hypotheses develops a habit of parallel or complex thought, so that "the mind appears to become possessed of the power of simultaneous vision from different standpoints." All this is tantamount to saying that the mind can pursue two (or more) lines of reasoning at the same time—a psychological impossibility. The fact is, that of multiple hypotheses only one can be used at a time. A selection must be made: one must be given priority. And that one will be tried out which seems most plausible. For the time it becomes the working hypothesis, though the others may remain on the threshold of consciousness, so to speak, as ready-made alternatives.

If all this is true, if multiple hypotheses can be used only one at a time, the question recurs: How can we guard against "the partiality of intellectual parentage"? There can be but one answer: by unswerving honesty. It is often said that science and history have nothing to do with ethics; and in a sense, the saying is true. The findings of science in themselves are ethically neutral; but if the scientist have not intellectual honesty, his output can never be trusted.

Darwin exemplified the perfectly correct attitude of the scientist. "I have steadily endeavored," he wrote, "to keep my mind free so as to give up any hypothesis, however much beloved (and I cannot resist forming one on every subject), as soon as facts are shown to be opposed to it. Indeed, I have had no choice but to act in this manner, for with the exception of the Coral Reefs, I cannot remember a single first-formed hypothesis which had not after a time to be given up or greatly modified." [1]

Unless a historian is content to be a mere annalist, putting his bits of information together like beads on a string, he will find some relationship between the events which describes. He will select a theme, or, if not a theme, then a period of history for investigation. For him that theme or period at once has a beginning, a middle, and an end. He will study his sources to elicit information which best explains beginning, middle, and end. If various explanations are possible, he will test one after another by painstaking reference to all the available data. These possible tentative explanations are alternative hypotheses: the reference to facts constitutes historical experimentation or verification.

The process is essentially that involved in all

[1] *Life and Letters* (1889), I, p. 83.

reflective thinking. Confronted by a puzzling situation which does not immediately explain itself, we "set our wits to work." Bewilderment may at first inhibit all coherent thought; then, feeling that we cannot have taken in the situation completely, we survey the details with some care, trying to discover new facts or incidents which may have been overlooked and which may hold the key to the problem. From this rapid inventory we may draw some hasty inferences, which we compare with our past experiences in similar situations or with what we know of the experiences of others. So far the process is mainly inductive. If we are clever enough or lucky enough, we may hit at once upon an "idea" that seems likely to explain the puzzling situation. The more we dwell upon it, the more it may seem to us an "inspiration," as we often say; but we are not content merely to hold this idea or concept. Plausible though it is, we do not know that it will bear a practical test. We are in doubt. We hold it in suspense. Then we turn back upon our course and again study the facts in the light of this newly born idea. We superimpose the general explanatory concept upon the facts—a deductive process. If it fails to meet the test completely, we reject it as no inspiration, after all, and try again. If it fits all the facts in the case and thus supplies a satisfactory explanation of all the puzzling details, we draw our conclusion. This, we say, is the real explanation; and our state of suspense ends.[1]

It goes without saying that the inductive and deductive processes occur almost simultaneously in consciousness, and that the whole mental process under ordinary circumstances is so rapid as to elude observation. "I do not know how I happened to think of it," is a frequent exclamation when we have stumbled upon some particularly happy solution of a difficult problem in practical life. Minds react at different speeds; and what we call intuition, which seems often at lightening speed to leap unerringly to the proper conclusion, is probably only an exceedingly rapid illustration of essentially the same process.

If now we substitute hypothesis for idea and concept in this description, we have all the essentials of scientific thinking. And if our description is correct, the forming of hypotheses is an in-

[1] The process is described with admirable clearness by John Dewey in his little book *How We Think.* For a more thorough-going discussion, the reader should go to *Studies in Logical Theory,* to which Dewey contributes the first four chapters on "Thought and Its Subject-matter."

dispensable part of the process, however much we may disguise it under every-day forms of speech. The whole process is so natural and logical that we are not wont to consider it in this formal way or in these scientific terms. Yet any one who will take the trouble to analyze the studies of a scrupulously accurate historian like Thucydides may assure himself that the process of arriving at the truth of events is fundamentally that of reflective thinking by the use of hypotheses.

When Thucydides avowed his theme to be the history of the war between the Peloponnesians and the Athenians, he encountered an initial difficulty: there was no general agreement as to the reasons for the breaking of the Thirty Years' Truce. Reflection upon the data which his researches had yielded led him, however, to a tentative explanation or hypothesis, which, put to the test of those facts, forced him to the conclusion that "the growth of the Athenian power was the truest occasion (of the war), though never openly avowed." And this conclusion he then proceeded to explain and justify by setting the alternative hypotheses before his readers, and showing how and why they did not fit the facts. "But the pretences, publicly alleged on either side for breaking the truce and declaring open war, shall now be related."

It may be said, however, that this part of the history of the Peloponnesian War lends itself readily to the use of hypotheses and that the narrative of military events presents no problems that require hypotheses. To a degree this is true. Ordinarily a simple narrative of events, when their chronological succession has been definitely fixed, can be carried forward without any hypothetical suppositions. It is only when doubts arise as to the dependence of event upon event, or when events are susceptible of different interpretations, or when a causal explanation of events is sought other than the obvious one, that reflective thinking begins. Hypothesis is born of doubt and uncertainty, and its function is to assist in the control and organization of confused data.

A careful survey and analysis of historical literature would show that historians make more frequent use of the hypothesis than perhaps either they or their readers are aware. A study or monograph which upsets a traditional view of some phase of history either by the discovery of new sources, or by a new interpretation of the old, is almost invariably founded upon a working hypothesis; and the monograph, stripped of its literary form and resolved into its logical components, consists of a detailed verification, or proof, of the validity of the hypothesis.

There is quite another way in which hypotheses appear in historiography. In a certain sense every writer of history has his own philosophy of history. Whether or no he is conscious of it, every historian writes with a predilection for one mode of interpretation or another. Freeman viewed history only as past politics; and nearly all English historians of the Victorian age shared his point of view. American historians from Bancroft to Rhodes riveted their attention usually upon political events—finding their themes either in the achievement of national independence and the making of the Union or in the Civil War. The progress of science, particularly of biological science, in the latter part of the nineteenth century, brought in a new conception of man and society, and gave emphasis to a wide variety of phenomena which historians had hitherto passed over with only casual attention. Monographic studies found favor in which this or that phase of human activity could be treated. Emphasis was laid upon the influence of geography, of climate, of physiography in general, upon history. A school of economic historians sprang up who pointed out the pressure of interests in determining group organizations. Intellectual movements were studied as highly interesting in themselves, whether or no they eventuated in action. The history of the sciences began to be written—of mathematics, of chemistry, of medicine. Anthropology brought new points of view; sociology suggested new syntheses; and now the new psychology offers novel ways and means of interpreting personality and behavior.[1]

The historical student of to-day, in short, can hardly avoid committing himself to some theory of history which will influence his choice and interpretation of material. Even when he risks the jibes of his contemporaries and deliberately turns to the themes of the old masters—the rise and development of states and the vicissitudes of political life—he finds himself facing stubborn social and economic facts which he cannot burke. He is forced to a new synthesis, whether he will or not. If he is prudent, he will first take counsel with himself and choose his point of view.

The writing of biography is passing through a

[1] *The New History and the Social Studies* (1925), by Harry E. Barnes, contains many thought-provoking hypotheses which historians would do well to test, whether or no they accept the writer's strictures on "the older historians."

critical period and calls for a choice of hypotheses. Few biographers now start out deliberately to imitate Carlyle. The age of hero-worship is gone. There never was a time, indeed, when the hero was conceived as a soul shaping absolutely its own destiny. "The man and his times" was the favorite theme—the individual coming first and receiving the larger share of attention. But interest centred in the will-attitudes of the man, in his reactions to circumstance. With the rise of economic determinism, the pendulum swung to the other extreme. The individual was conceived as a mere plaything of mighty economic forces, rising to view if he swam with the current, submerged if he swam against it. Motives are of secondary interest, for motives are now held to be merely attempts to rationalize conduct; instincts and interests are primary concerns. Not as a man thinketh, so is he, but as he feels. The Holy Writ expresses a true psychology when it declares that where a man's treasure is, there will his heart be also. To such determinists the older biography, which depicted the individual as a St. George wrestling victoriously with the dragon of fell circumstance, appears childishly futile, while the writings of Sainte-Beuve and his modern imitators seem no better than flights of fancy.

Biography appears in a new light, however, to the modern Freudian. Fortified by his examination of clinical cases, the psychiatrist or the psychoanalyst is prepared to interpret human behavior in new terms. When the determinist declares that circumstances shape conduct, the psychoanalyst asks: "What circumstances?" Assuredly not merely those of the outward, physical environment. There are things not dreamed of in that determinist philosophy. You must search for the facts of heredity, of prenatal life, of infancy, of puberty. These are the formative years of personality. In them are accumulated the emotional experiences which lead to repressions and indulgences, which give rise to complexes, which fix character-patterns.

The biographer now has at his disposal, too, ready-made categories of personality. Following Jung, he may catalogue his subject as an extrovert or as an introvert; or he may put him among the stable-minded or unstable-minded, as Trotter formulates the fundamental contrasting types.[1] As hypotheses for the explanation of persistent behavior in historical characters, these type-patterns may have value; but it may be questioned whether the data are available for any

[1] Jung, *Analytical Psychology*, chap. XI. W. Trotter, *The Instincts of the Herd in Peace and War*, chap. II.

such positive conclusions as the exponents of the new psychology demand of historians and biographers.

It is perhaps not unfitting that a book on historical method and evidence should end in an admonitory vein. Historians owe much to the social sciences, no doubt, but the obligation is reciprocal. The social sciences were founded on data furnished by historical research, and they cannot remain indifferent to the critical processes by which that material was obtained. There are cogent reasons for believing, moreover, that historians will continue to furnish data which political scientists, anthropologists, economists, and sociologists will need increasingly. It may well be that historians need a wider point of view—perhaps new points of view—and that they would profit by using the hypotheses suggested by the social sciences; but more than ever they must weigh evidence with meticulous care. The more daring and the more promising the hypotheses, the greater the obligation to tell the truth, the whole truth, and nothing but the truth.

INDEX

INDEX

INDEX